CONTENTS

PREFACE
A New Generation of Mathematics Curricula

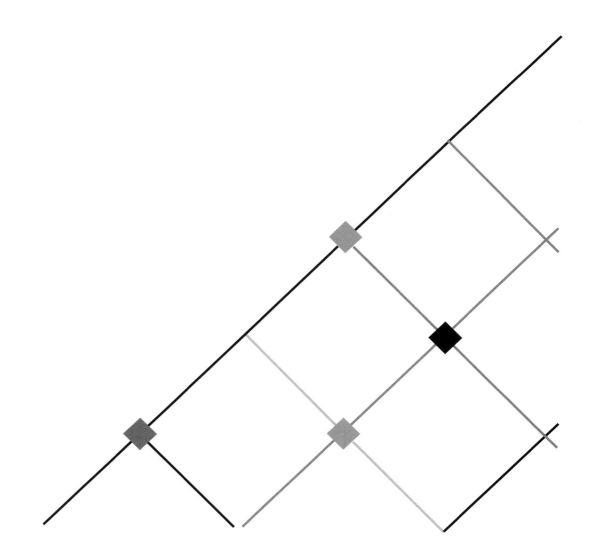

PREFACE

A New Generation of Mathematics Curricula

If your district is preparing to review mathematics curricula for adoption, you are standing at a moment of opportunity. The past decade has been a time of great activity in mathematics education, and one of the results has been the creation of a number of new curricula designed to promote a deeper and richer kind of mathematical learning for students.

As you plan for a new round of adoption for your district, you are in a position to make decisions that can help improve your mathematics programs. The availability of these new curricula means that you have more choices about how students in your district will learn mathematics. You can use this adoption cycle to engage in communitywide conversations about the kind of mathematics education you want your students to receive. In this way you can transform a routine district activity—updating your mathematics program—into an affirmation of your community's goals for mathematics education and a careful consideration of the curricula that best support those goals.

> It's easy to work through a curriculum selection process in a very mechanical and routine way and not learn something about the nature of instruction or our commitment to principles and concepts. We **did** come through this process with a bigger vision of what we want for kids and a bigger vision for the school system. (J.G., assistant superintendent for curriculum and instruction)

What are the changes in mathematics education all about? The publication of three key documents nearly a decade ago by the National Council of Teachers of Mathematics (NCTM) articulated a perspective on mathematics learning, teaching, and assessment that challenged the traditional emphasis on "shopkeeper's arithmetic" and routine problem solving.[1] According to this new perspective, the global transformation from an industry-based society to an information-based one has involved a corresponding transformation of expectations for mathematical literacy. The mathematical competence necessary for success in the information age includes the familiar fluency with facts and skills, but it also requires sophisticated mathematical reasoning and problem solving in a variety of contexts. The perspective articulated in the NCTM *Standards* challenges the widely-held assumption that mathematical thinking is accessible to only a talented few and emphasizes the importance of educating *all* students to become mathematical thinkers.

---

[1] These three documents, *Curriculum and Evaluation Standards for School Mathematics* (published in 1989), *Professional Standards for Teaching Mathematics* (published in 1991), and *Assessment Standards for School Mathematics* (published in 1995), are generally considered to represent leading mathematics educators' visions of mathematics teaching and learning. A revision of these documents (called *Principles and Standards for School Mathematics*) is currently underway, due to be released in the year 2000. While the revision will preserve the fundamental message of the original documents, it will also incorporate feedback that is based on a decade of experience translating this message into classroom practice.

In the intervening decade, many states and local districts have crafted supplementary frameworks, based on the NCTM *Standards*, that reflect the particulars of their own state or community goals. Taken together, these standards and frameworks lay out a vision of mathematics education that reflects much of the current thinking about best practices, and guides the work of many curriculum developers, teacher educators, and classroom teachers.

During this time a number of curriculum development teams have created mathematics programs intended to reflect the new emphases of the NCTM *Standards*. The increasing availability of these materials has facilitated many districts' moves toward reform-minded mathematics instruction. These curricula are based on the premise that students should be "doing" mathematics: learning important mathematical concepts, acquiring mathematical skills, and developing methods for investigating mathematical ideas.

Curriculum or Program?

What's the difference between a curriculum and a program? Taken most broadly, a **curriculum** refers to the ideas, skills, and dispositions that educators and content specialists identify as the important ones for students to learn. States and districts are developing **curriculum frameworks** which articulate these learning goals. (Districts may further refine this articulation by indicating the concepts and skills to be learned at each grade level.) **Curriculum materials**—the written lessons, activities, exercises, and supporting materials—provide the means through which teachers engage student learning, offering teachers a structure and organization for instruction, as well as the important content to teach. Districts build their **programs** by selecting curriculum materials that will help them meet their curricular goals.

Sometimes the available curriculum materials only address portions of the overall curriculum. In these cases, the district's program is composed of a collection of different materials. This has often been the case in such subject areas as language arts and science; it has less often been true for mathematics. (If, however, your district has adopted a mathematics textbook that teachers have been supplementing with lessons focusing on inquiry, or if teachers are adding skills-based lessons to inquiry-based texts, then teachers have constructed programs on their own that use a variety of materials to address the district's curriculum.)

In practical terms, when you look to mathematics materials designed to address the NCTM *Standards*, the distinction between "curriculum" and "program" becomes very subtle. These materials were developed to be comprehensive programs of study that meet the goals of a standards-based curriculum. Because of this close match, we use the words "curriculum" and "program" interchangeably in this guide.

This focus on students' sense-making has led developers to create programs that often look quite different from the traditional mathematics textbook. The familiar "flip test" strategy, which provides a quick and reasonable fix on the differences between texts that present generally the same topics in the same way and in the same order, offers very little information about how standards-based curricula develop mathematical ideas and skills. The lessons in these new curricula often integrate several mathematical topics or skills, extend over several class periods, and embed skill mastery and practice within other activities. The experience of learning to review standards-based curricula led one assistant superintendent for curriculum and instruction to observe, "It requires education to understand the value of the new materials. We have to be given new eyes, new yardsticks, and new noses to sniff out the good in the packaged stuff."

About This Guide

This guide describes the "eyes, yardsticks, and noses" that will help you consider your community's goals for mathematics education, evaluate curricula, and plan a successful adoption process. As a publication of the National Science Foundation-funded K–12 Mathematics Curriculum Center, this guide focuses on the 13 programs supported by the Center, though many of the ideas we discuss are not specific to these particular programs (see Appendices 1 and 2 for listings of the specific curricula and the implementation centers that support them).

This guide also addresses issues involved in curriculum selection and implementation and offers ideas to help you work through both of these phases. Our focus for the selection phase is on assembling a selection committee, assessing resources and needs, and creating guidelines and criteria for evaluating different programs. The curriculum implementation section focuses on ways districts can work toward successful use of the materials they have purchased—planning a realistic and effective roll-out strategy, supporting teachers, and building community buy-in and assistance.

In designing and organizing the guide we have made decisions about order and presentation that are based on our goals for its use. Because we believe that you will be able to make more informed decisions about how to use the guide if our own decisions about its content and organization are made explicit, we briefly describe below the rationale for our approach.

Comprehensiveness

This guide presents a comprehensive view of selection and implementation. It is more of an ideal view than a picture of how any individual district goes about adopting new mathematics curricula. Our purpose is to convey a range of issues you may confront, decisions you will have to make, and strategies you may choose, and to offer a variety of procedures and processes that others have found useful.

Given the large number of school districts in the country, no two will encounter exactly the same issues or resolve problems in exactly the same ways. Each has its own particular setting, situation, and story. While there are common threads running through districts' experiences with selecting and implementing standards-based mathematics curricula, the individuality of each district's circumstances also make the particulars of their processes unique. By offering an inclusive account we hope to provide many districts with a point of entry into the process and some guidance on ways to proceed. In writing this guide we have drawn on the experiences of a number of diverse districts across the country, creating a cumulative account of their processes for selecting and implementing standards-based curricula. We have included quotes and examples in the text to give you an idea of how aspects of these processes have played out in particular contexts.

The particulars of your own district will probably make some parts of this guide more useful or relevant to you than others. We have found that many districts experience some kind of catalyst for curricular and instructional change but that these catalysts can be quite distinct. The particular catalyst that sets the process into motion also determines which issues are seen as most important as the process unfolds. For example, in some districts the catalyst is the desire to improve test scores, while in others it is the search for curricula to complement programs already in use at other grade levels. In the former districts the focus may be on assessment issues, while in the latter the focus is on the treatment of mathematical skills and concepts at different grade levels. In some districts, teachers' interest in standards-based curriculum and instruction spearheads the process, and the focus is on community buy-in. In others the opposite situation prevails—the administration hopes to promote teacher interest in new curricula, and the focus is on teachers' professional development.

The specific reasons that initially bring you to the search for a standards-based curriculum and the particulars of your district will determine those selection and implementation issues that will be most salient for you. These will, in large measure, shape your journey through the process itself. You can use this guide to identify and focus on those aspects of the process that will be most central to your own situation, doing a more cursory reading of those sections dealing with aspects of the process that are less germane.

Representing the Process as Linear

We have chosen to lay out the selection and implementation process more or less chronologically, even though it actually won't unfold in a strictly linear fashion in your district. Parts of the process need not have a strictly specified order (e.g., conducting a needs and resources assessment could either precede or follow the creation of a selection committee). Parts of the process can be concurrent (e.g., roughing out a budget and reviewing curricula). Other parts of the process are interconnected in complex ways (e.g., piloting different curricula can inform both selection and implementation). Because different aspects of these processes may overlap in time or be interconnected, you may find yourself doubling back to earlier sections of the guide or skipping ahead.

Dual Focus

This guide balances two foci—paying attention to the big picture of selecting and implementing standards-based curricula, and dealing with the logistics of an adoption cycle. We have generally sought to integrate these two foci, discussing goals and rationales for different activities while offering practical suggestions for how to accomplish each task. As you reach different points in your own process, you may find it most useful to read the guide through one or the other of these two lenses.

The next two chapters offer a brief overview of the principles behind standards-based curricula and a look at the "big ideas" of the selection and implementation process.

PART I
Background

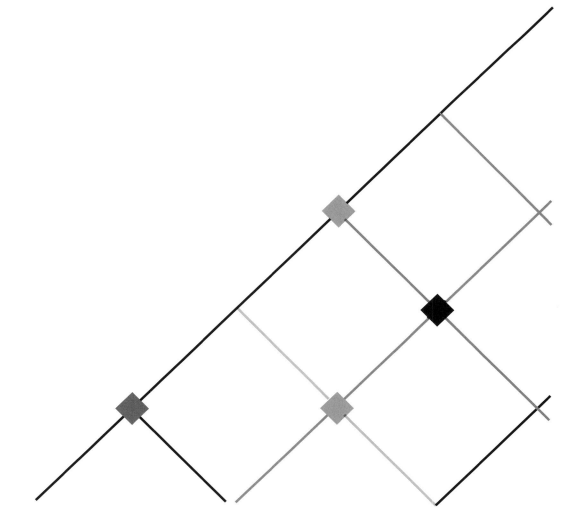

8

CHAPTER 1

What Is a Standards-Based Curriculum?

Talk about "the *Standards*" is everywhere. You hear about them when you go to conferences, read professional publications, receive guidelines from your state department of education, talk with colleagues in the teachers' lounge, and discuss curriculum options with publishers. While people often talk about the *Standards*, it is not always clear what they mean. Different people focus on different aspects of the *Standards* and may interpret them differently as well.

The NCTM has presented a view of mathematics learning, teaching, and assessment that shifts the focus away from memorization and rote application of procedures toward standards for performance that are based on conceptual understanding and reasoning. There are several forces promoting this shift, including recent advances in theories of learning and the dawning of the information age. The NCTM developed a set of national standards for curriculum, instruction, and assessment in order to answer several questions:

- What do we want students to know about mathematics, and what should they be able to do?

- How do we determine when students know the mathematics we want them to know?

- What mathematics do we want teachers to know and be able to do?

The responses to these questions are contained in the three *Standards* documents referred to in the Preface, representing the consensus of leading mathematics educators nationwide. These documents are based on a set of beliefs about mathematics as a body of knowledge and about the learning processes that lead to mathematical understanding. Briefly, these beliefs include the following:

- Mathematical literacy is essential to becoming an informed and competent citizen.

- All students can (and should) become mathematically literate, not just those students who have traditionally performed well in mathematics classes.

- Literacy involves understanding mathematical principles (such as change, function, and quantitative relationships), developing mathematical ways of thinking, and developing fluency with number, geometry, and data.

- Students develop this literacy by actively doing mathematics—using their skills and knowledge to solve problems and investigate mathematical ideas.

Many leading mathematics educators interpret the relatively poor showing of U.S. students in the recent Third International Mathematics and Science Study

(TIMSS) as evidence of the need for a change toward standards-based mathematics instruction. They argue that student performance on the TIMSS evaluations indicates a weakness in students' conceptual understanding and mathematical reasoning abilities, and that one source of this weakness is the curriculum, which has been described as "a mile wide and an inch deep."

In an effort to create classroom materials teachers could use to promote deeper and more substantial mathematical understanding in their students, developers of standards-based curricula grounded their work in the core beliefs outlined above. Building from these principles, different curriculum developers have emphasized somewhat different aspects of the *Standards* and have taken somewhat different approaches in their materials. For example, some programs place a heavy emphasis on student discourse, some use applications to motivate the mathematics in the curriculum, some embed skill development within the context of real-world problem solving, and some include more explicit practice. The result is a collection of mathematics programs that bear a "family resemblance" to one another because they are based on a common set of core beliefs, but which also represent distinctive interpretations of those beliefs.

A large number of currently available curricula describe themselves as "standards-based," and even a cursory examination of the presentation of materials will confirm that virtually every text looks different than those of 30, or 20, or even 10 years ago. All but the most traditional of today's textbooks offer sections on problem solving, include applied problems that involve practical uses for the mathematics students are learning, cover mathematical topics that were not part of textbooks 15 years ago, and presume that their users will come from a variety of backgrounds, bringing a range of learning styles to the mathematics classroom. Yet there is a significant difference between texts that have retrofitted their traditional "demonstration and practice" approaches in order to better align themselves with the NCTM *Standards*, and curricula that were designed from the outset to embody the mathematical approaches and pedagogical principles advanced by the *Standards*.

This section reviews the key aspects of the NCTM *Standards* that relate to curricula, in order to help you recognize the differences between curricula in which the goals and values of the *Standards* are integral to the fundamental design and current curricula that have imported some of the activities and instructional techniques associated with the reform movement.

The *Standards* identify four essential aspects of mathematics education and articulate goals for each of them with respect to curricula. The four aspects are:

- mathematical content
- mathematical processes
- attitudes toward mathematics
- views of teaching and learning

Following is a brief explanation of each, along with some implications for the teaching of mathematics.

Mathematical Content

First and foremost, the *Standards* are about the ideas and skills that children should acquire during their K–12 mathematics education. The *Standards* stress the importance of helping students develop deep conceptual understanding, fluency with skill-based manipulations, and the ability to reason and communicate about mathematical ideas. They emphasize the understanding of underlying mathematical concepts and the connections among them—the "big ideas" of mathematics that children learn over a long period of time, across topics and units. Curricula can support student understanding by drawing connections among mathematical ideas and between mathematics and everyday experiences, rather than by presenting mathematics as a set of discrete, unrelated topics that students learn, forget after the test, and then (perhaps) relearn the next year.

This perspective on the importance of conceptual understanding and the connectedness of mathematical ideas led the authors of the *Standards* to recommend less rote learning. For example, they advocate spending less time teaching such procedures as long division or the factoring of polynomials and place a greater emphasis on spatial reasoning, understanding probability, and reasoning about data. These changes are motivated by beliefs about the kinds of mathematical skills and understanding that will be needed for life and work in the twenty-first century.

Big Ideas

"Big ideas" in mathematics are those ideas and principles that govern the structure and functioning of the mathematical system. When students understand these "big ideas," they have the conceptual tools to approach and solve many different kinds of problems. One of the fundamental ideas of algebra, for example, is that you can operate on an unknown number as if it were known. The ability to think about mathematical relationships in terms of the general case allows students to summarize observations, make predictions, and develop such proofs as the following:

Prove that the sum of any two consecutive numbers is odd.

If the first of the two consecutive numbers is n, then the second is n + 1.

The sum of the two numbers is n + n + 1, or 2n + 1.

2n is even, regardless of the value of n.

Adding 1 to any even number yields an odd number, so the sum of any two consecutive numbers must be odd.

Some have interpreted the *Standards'* emphasis on conceptual understanding to mean that they do not recommend traditional skill mastery. This is not the case. The *Standards* do *not* contend that computation is unimportant or that students can get by without knowing basic number facts and operations. They do, however, recommend diminishing the amount of class time spent on strictly rote skills development (the "drill and kill" approach) in order to make more room for conceptually-based learning. Some of the newer programs embed mastery of skills in games or activities that also target other kinds of thinking (for example, developing strategic thinking or number sense). Because skill mastery is somewhat hidden in these contexts, someone who is unaccustomed to recognizing the skill component of standards-based curricula may have the impression that skills and facts are not being taught.

Below is a list of the general content areas recommended in the original *Standards* document. For a more detailed version, see the *Curriculum and Evaluation Standards for School Mathematics*. Note also that the upcoming revision, *Principles and Standards for School Mathematics*, will include changes in recommendations about specific mathematical strands. What will not change is the emphasis on developing solid understanding of important mathematical concepts, rather than a passing familiarity with many mathematical topics.

GRADES K–4 CONTENT AREAS	GRADES 5–8 CONTENT AREAS	GRADES 9–12 CONTENT AREAS
Number Operations/ Computation	Number Operations/ Computation	Algebra
Geometry/Measurement	Geometry/Measurement	Geometry
Probability/Statistics	Probability	Trigonometry
Patterns/Relationships	Statistics	Functions
	Algebra	Statistics
		Probability
		Discrete Mathematics

One criticism of the *Standards* is that the recommendations simply add new areas to an already long list of topics to teach. Developers of new standards-based programs have sought to focus on the most important mathematical ideas, choosing topics that support their development. Nonetheless, your district will need to have a clear sense of the mathematics you want your students to learn so that you can examine potential curricula in this light. Reviewing your district's current curriculum scope and sequence, the kinds of assessments your students must take, and relevant standards and frameworks (which may include national, state, and/or local documents) can help you decide on the content that is most important for your students to master.

Mathematical Processes

Students gain mathematical competence by learning to think about mathematics and communicate their ideas to others. In addition to mastering skills and concepts (the major focus of traditional mathematics education), students should be engaging in a variety of mathematical processes. The *Standards* outline four processes that promote mathematical thinking across the grade levels and which should be a fundamental part of mathematics education:

1. **Problem solving.** The *Standards* recommend that students learn to develop and apply strategies for investigating mathematical content and solving problems. It also is important that problem solving be contextualized, that is, that the problems be motivated by situations and applications that give them meaning.

2. **Communication.** The *Standards* emphasize the importance of written and verbal communication. Expecting students to convey their mathematical ideas to others encourages students to reason clearly, articulate their thinking and justify it to others.

3. **Mathematical reasoning.** There is great value placed on learning to think logically and critically about mathematics from the very earliest grades. The emphasis on reasoning about mathematical situations begins with students recognizing and effectively using different problem-solving strategies in the early elementary grades, and leads to students employing both inductive and deductive reasoning by high school.

4. **Connections.** The *Standards* also emphasize the importance of learning to make connections, both within mathematics and between mathematics and the world. Students should make connections between different mathematical strands, different representations or models for the same mathematical relationships, particular examples and general mathematical principles, personal experiences and mathematical situations, and practical problems and mathematical solutions.

In order to give you a flavor of the kind of thinking that the *Standards* seek to encourage, we have included an excerpt of a classroom vignette written by a fourth grade teacher. In this excerpt the teacher describes a conversation she had with one of her students, a young girl named April, as April posed and solved a division problem. As you read this vignette, look for the ways that April works to understand division—thinking about groups of objects, finding upper and lower bounds for her answer, breaking down the original problem into more manageable units, and using diagrams to visualize a solution. Be aware as well of how the teacher works to understand April's thinking and to help her continue developing her solution.

> [April] started off by saying that "you have to know multiplication [to do division]" . . . I asked her to work on another problem so she could talk a little more about how her strategy developed . . . She decided to use jelly beans (being Easter and all!) again and make the problem a little harder.

Divide 143 jelly beans among 8 kids.

I asked April to tell me first what she did when she was dividing. She said that division was putting things into groups. "You have to multiply the things to get the groups—like take 8 times any number and see what the answer is." She began her strategy by saying that she knew each kid would get more than 10 jelly beans because that would be 80, and that if each kid got 20 jelly beans, that would be 160, which was too much. So she knew two things: that 10 was too small and 20 was too big. I asked if she thought the correct number would be closer to 10 or closer to 20. She said she thought it would be around 14, and proceeded to multiply 14 x 8, 112. She then said that you had to add 31 more. She then decided to try 22 x 8 and got 176. She said she knew she had to try a number that would bring her close to the 160 mark, but lower.

April now decided to "bag" this idea and came up with another strategy—to see how many eights were in 100, and then how many eights were in 43—to see if that worked. Her process:

10 x 8 = 80, 11 x 8 = 88, 12 x 8 = 96 (with 4 left)
5 x 8 = 40 (with 3 left)

The next part she struggled with. She was losing her train of thought and was confused by all the numbers she had just generated. I tried to help her sort out what she had done by showing her that she had found 12 groups of 8 in 100 and 5 groups of 8 in 40, and that in both cases she had numbers left over. I asked her to think about how many groups of 8 she had. She had 17 groups of 8 (which totaled 136) with 7 jelly beans left over . . .

Then she came up with a way to divide up the 7 extra jelly beans. She took 4 of them and divided each in half, so each of the 8 kids got 1/2. Then she had 3 left over, so she took 2 of those and divided them into fourths, so each kid got an additional 1/4. Then she divided the last jelly bean into eighths, so each kid got another 1/8.

Now the question was how much was 1/2 + 1/4 + 1/8? This is how she solved that problem.

April was delighted when she saw that 1/8 was left over; she immediately knew that the total was 7/8. In the end, each kid got 17 7/8 jelly beans.[2]

---

[2] From *Developing Mathematical Ideas: Number and Operations: Building a System of Tens* © 1999 by the Education Development Center, Inc. Published by Dale Seymour Publications, an imprint of Pearson Learning. Used by permission.

By emphasizing the development of mathematical processes, the *Standards* stress the importance of developing mathematical thinking by engaging in mathematical work. A number of years ago, chess Life Master John Collins talked about a "chessical" way of thinking—the ability to read a board, have a certain appreciation for the flow of play, and command the interplay of strategy and tactic. Chess players learn to think chessically by immersing themselves in the play and study of chess. Similarly, students develop mathematical ways of thinking by immersing themselves in the exploration and study of mathematics.

When these content and process *Standards* are taken together, they point to a very different kind of mathematics curriculum—one that is organized to address the development of conceptual, as well as procedural, understanding; follows the thread of ideas through mathematical strands; poses different kinds of problems to students; and promotes a different kind of problem solving. As you review standards-based programs, you are likely to find that they have the following features:

- There is a more integrated approach to topics, with several areas of mathematics appearing at each grade level and developing in connection to each other rather than in isolation. Students work on ideas about number, function, geometry, and data from kindergarten on. This is particularly noticeable at the high school level, where the traditional Algebra I–Geometry–Algebra II–Trigonometry/PreCalculus series has been modified to create a more interconnected and integrated sequence of mathematical topics throughout grades 9–12.

- Topics reappear at different grade levels in increasingly sophisticated forms. For example, early elementary-level lessons on probability and statistics focus on ideas of chance, developing in later grades into the study of fairness and statistics; elementary grades' work with patterns evolves toward a more formal study of algebraic relationships in middle and high school.

- Mathematical knowledge is developed within practical and conceptual contexts. There is less work with "naked numbers"—decontextualized problems whose goal is symbol or number manipulation—and more work that connects problems to other mathematical ideas and the world.

- Many problems are complex, requiring a number of mathematical ideas and skills and taking more time and thought to solve than the problems of the past.

- There is an emphasis on using different kinds of representations, such as charts, tables, graphs, diagrams, and formal notation, for exploring, describing, and testing problem situations.

- Teachers and students take on different roles in the classroom as more of the learning occurs through exploration and discussion of mathematical ideas. Students make conjectures and investigate them, explain their reasoning, and work individually and in groups to solve problems.

• Teachers lecture less and listen more for students' ideas, ask questions designed to clarify and extend students' thinking, and pose new questions or activities to further their understanding.

Attitudes Toward Mathematics

> "I have horrid memories of learning mathematics as a youngster. I can vividly recall crying my eyes out because I couldn't do long division."
>
> "I've never liked math. A lot of it has to do with self-confidence. I never felt I really understood math. I just did what it took to get by."
>
> "I hated math as a kid. I got math facts wrong. I didn't understand what was going on. Algebra was a mysterious language that was undecipherable."

It's not unusual for people to associate their experiences as mathematics learners with confusion, uncertainty, and discomfort and to think of themselves as deficient mathematics learners. In fact, many adults recall with relief the day they endured their last mathematics class. Recently we asked a group of people in their twenties, thirties, and forties to write mathematics autobiographies; two-thirds of them wrote with surprising intensity about their negative experiences and feelings!

The *Standards* call for education that will create a positive shift in attitudes about mathematics for all students. Instead of developing the belief that mathematics is mysterious, if not downright unfathomable, students should come to think of mathematics as an interesting, sensible, and useful body of knowledge.

Equity in mathematical mastery is another major goal of standards-based curricula. Historically, mathematics has often been considered a subject that is understood by a select, especially talented few. The *Standards* take a contrary view, emphasizing the critical importance of making mathematics accessible to *all* students—those who have traditionally excelled and those who have struggled or simply tuned out. The *Standards* call for engaging all students in educational experiences that will enable them to recognize and value the power of their own mathematical thinking.

The developers of standards-based curricula have sought to address issues of equity in a number of ways. At a superficial level, they have depicted people from different racial and ethnic groups and people with disabilities within the materials themselves. More substantively, they have worked to create lessons that have multiple entry points, allowing students with different levels of mathematical sophistication and different learning styles to find ways to engage with the mathematical ideas (for an example, see the "Crossing the River" problem in the box below). Developers have also sought to motivate mathematical work by presenting problem contexts that students are likely to find interesting and compelling.

Crossing the River

There are eight adults and two children having a picnic on the banks of the Lazy Horse River. They finish their picnic and want to go exploring on the other side of the river. They have one small boat and everyone can row it. It can hold one adult, or two children at a time. It can also hold just one child. The river isn't very wide or

---

very deep and the children are good rowers, so it's okay for them to row back and forth on their own.

> A. How many one-way trips does it take for the entire group to cross the river?

> B. How many trips would it take for 2 children and 100 adults?

> C. Describe how you would figure it out for 2 children and any number of adults.

Below are solutions from three middle-grade students. These solutions illustrate different approaches to the problem, all of which yield the correct answer. Students generally devised a strategy to solve the initial problem (part A) and then generalized this strategy to construct their own rule to solve the extensions of the problem (parts B and C). In the first solution, the student describes a rule for counting the total number of trips. The second solution uses a traditional algebraic representation, while the third student describes the solution with a diagram and written explanation.

Solution 1:

One student answered part B as follows:

"It takes four trips to get 1 adult across the river. And one additional trip for the children to get across the last time. For 100 adults to get across the river (including 2 kids) it would take 401 total one-way trips."

Solution 2:

In solving part A, the student answers, "Begin with 3 trips to get 1 adult over. Each additional [adult] is four trips." Then she constructs her rule for part C by stating, "Subtract 1 from the total number of adults. Multiply that answer by 4. Add three to the total of that. Add two to get the kids across and there's your answer!

   (A-1) * 4 + 3 + 2 = ___ "

Solution 3:

This student answers part B by describing an algorithm and illustrating it with a diagram:

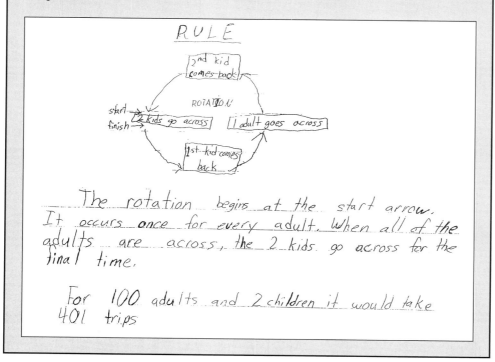

RULE

2nd kid comes-back

ROTATION

start / finish → 2 kids go across   1 adult goes across

1st kid comes back

The rotation begins at the start arrow. It occurs once for every adult. When all of the adults are across, the 2 kids go across for the final time.

For 100 adults and 2 children it would take 401 trips

Views of Learning and Teaching

The *Standards* take a view of learning and teaching that adds certain dimensions to traditional mathematics instruction. The emphasis on engaging students in *doing* mathematics—making connections, problem solving, reasoning, and communicating—is intended to help students understand the *why* as well as the *how* of the mathematics they study.

This emphasis on students' active learning derives from the fact that learners *construct* their own understanding through their experiences with mathematical problems and discussions with teachers, parents, and peers. They are naturally driven to use their current knowledge and understanding to make sense of situations and work toward accurate and efficient problem solving.

In order to support students' construction of deep and flexible understanding of mathematical content, the *Standards* recommend that students of all ages do the following:

- interact with a range of materials for representing problem situations, such as manipulatives, calculators, computers, diagrams, tables, and charts

- work collaboratively as well as individually

- focus on making sense of the mathematics they are studying as well as learning to achieve accurate and efficient solutions to problems

These recommendations mean that instruction in a standards-based classroom has a flow and focus that may be unfamiliar to teachers. Classrooms are often busy—students talk with the teacher and with each other (sometimes even debating heatedly), leave their seats to get materials or to consult with others, cover their desks with the materials they need to represent problem situations, explain and defend their ideas, and sometimes work on problems over an extended period of time (days, or even weeks). Children may approach the same problem in very different ways, sharing and comparing their various strategies. There is more action and noise and, to an unaccustomed eye, such a classroom may look bustling—perhaps even unfocused. After some practice, however, it's possible to recognize busy, but nonetheless purposeful, learning.

Teachers, too, have different roles in standards-based classrooms. They listen closely to their students' ideas, analyzing them to learn where student understanding is firm and where it is still developing. They use this careful listening, along with their knowledge of how children's mathematical thinking develops, to plan lessons to move their students' understanding forward. Teachers are more aware of the need to ask questions that will lead in mathematically productive directions and to give their students the space to think through ideas on their own. The curriculum materials themselves can help prepare teachers for these roles and responsibilities, but they cannot script the conversations or prescribe the implementation strategies that will guarantee student learning.

Teachers in standards-based classrooms must become more alert to student thinking, more cognizant of the "big ideas" that underlie the mathematics they teach, and more focused on helping students understand and apply these ideas. For many teachers, developing these skills and strategies will require time and support through professional development.

Summary

Standards-based curricula are built around the principles and perspectives articulated in the NCTM *Standards* documents, which include the importance of the following:

- mathematical content
- mathematical processes
  - ~ problem solving
  - ~ communication
  - ~ mathematical reasoning
  - ~ connections
- attitudes toward mathematics
- views of teaching and learning

Curricula that are developed around these principles differ from conventional programs in both their approach to the mathematical content and their pedagogical stance. Learning to evaluate standards-based curricula, therefore, involves learning to look at materials differently.

CHAPTER 2

Getting Started: The "Big Ideas" of the Selection and Implementation Process

Any one of a variety of factors may set an adoption process in motion, for example, the budget cycle, community dissatisfaction over poor student achievement tests, state-level mandates for new curriculum adoptions, outdated textbooks, or the reform-minded vision of a small group of teachers and administrators. Districts generally begin to organize the process around this initial need, branching out to consider other issues as the process continues. Whatever the factors that bring you to consider standards-based curricula for your next adoption, you will need to know what to expect when reviewing standards-based materials so that you can lay out a realistic timeline and initial plan of action. You also will need to know how the process will be similar to other adoptions you have been through, and how it will be different.

> We broke with tradition in our recent middle grades mathematics curriculum materials selection process. Previously, a small committee of teachers would sit around a table for three days listening to presentations from publishers, review materials for three months, come back together to make a decision, and the curriculum would be implemented the following year. This process was not going to work with the reform curricula. There needed to be large-scale buy-in. Teachers needed to have in-depth experiences with the materials. They needed some training. (D.B., mathematics curriculum consultant)

In our talks with district mathematics leaders throughout the country, several common issues and challenges have emerged. To help you get oriented and begin with your planning, we have distilled their experiences into six guiding principles—big ideas—for adopting standards-based curricula. You will encounter these principles throughout this guide.

Think Long Term

No matter how you end up working through the particulars of the selection and implementation process, chances are that both phases will take longer than they have in the past. There are several reasons you likely will need an extended timetable. For example, your district may need to raise general awareness (and support) among teachers, administrators, and parents for the goals and methods of standards-based mathematics education. Also, the review process itself will take longer. Because the mathematical ideas in standards-based curricula are generally presented within the context of activities and problems, you will have to examine the materials more carefully to get a sense of how the curriculum will work in the classroom. While you might be able to tell how the mathematics develops in some textbooks by reading the table of contents and browsing quickly through a unit or two, this strategy does not work very well with many of the standards-based curricula. With unit names like "All About Alice" and "Going the Distance," it is not immediately apparent what mathematical ideas form the basis of each lesson.

The implementation process will also take longer. Unless the teachers in your district have already been using innovative activities with their students and are therefore familiar with the kinds of teaching demands they will encounter with standards-based curricula, they will need more time to learn to use the new curriculum than if they were simply upgrading from one edition of a textbook to the next. Teachers may find both the pedagogical orientation of standards-based programs and some of the mathematics content to be unfamiliar. Some districts decide to extend the implementation process itself, phasing it in along with professional development designed to help teachers learn to use the materials effectively.

> You also have to instill in teachers [that] it's going to take them 5–6 years to become skilled teachers of the program. Like a skilled artisan given new, sophisticated equipment, they're not going to get it right away—they'll need time. They must understand that, and we as administrators must also know that and give them time and support. (C.U., associate superintendent for curriculum and instruction)

Take a K-12 Perspective

Whether you will be selecting a standards-based curriculum at a single grade level or across the K–12 grade span, it is important to think about how your mathematics programs fit together at the different grade levels and how they fit with your district's curriculum framework. Taking a K–12 perspective will help you to minimize areas of overlap and redress gaps in content at the transitions between grade levels. This perspective will also help give you an overview of the pedagogical approaches used at different grade levels, and will help you prepare teachers and students for possible discontinuity in classroom structure and instructional approaches at these transition points. It can also help you to plan for conversations among teachers at different grade levels so they can have a better grasp of students' experiences in these transitions.

Know Your District's Current Situation

It is important to have a realistic assessment of the current levels of experience with standards-based mathematics education within the district, and of the degree of commitment (or even interest) among teachers, administrators, parents, and other community members. As a community, you will need to look at where you are at the moment, agree on where you want mathematics education to be in the future, and develop a plan for bridging the gap. A vision for mathematics education in the future and a realistic assessment of the current conditions in your district are crucial for your planning and decision making. You will use changes in curriculum and instruction to move toward your goal, making choices and allocating resources based on assessments of how much of the gap you can bridge at a time.

Identify people both inside and outside of your district who can help move your mathematics education agenda forward, and cultivate new relationships that will do the same. The more you can call on members of the community for expertise and support, the more the community will be able to work together to make your curriculum adoption successful. It is also important to make connections with people in other districts that have adopted standards-based curricula. Their experiences and perspectives can help alert you to important issues and point you toward available resources, and they may have practical advice about the selection and implementation process.

Cultivate New Ideas about Mathematics, Teaching, and Learning

Taking a standards-based view of mathematics education means changing ideas about teaching, learning, and curriculum. Sometimes people interpret the *Standards* in terms of activities or behaviors, for example, using manipulatives or asking students to explain their thinking. While these are means by which reformers' ideas about teaching and learning are put into practice, they do not by themselves guarantee that powerful mathematical understanding will result. Learning to recognize quality in new programs and in their implementation involves developing new expectations for mathematics teaching and learning:

- Understand mathematical concepts.

- Develop facility with mathematical skills in order to engage in higher-order reasoning and problem-solving.

- Engage in sustained mathematical inquiry and problem solving.

- Work collectively as well as individually.

- Communicate ideas with others.

> Lots of people think that reform is about the trappings—working in groups, having "problems of the week," using portfolios—and they don't get the **spirit** of the reform, which is that math education is about thinking mathematically. (G.T., middle school teacher leader)

Build Stakeholder Support and Commitment

Districts that have recently adopted standards-based programs consistently note that stakeholders' commitment to the curriculum is central to its successful implementation. It is important to have the support of a variety of stakeholder groups, from those who are most directly affected by the introduction of a new program (classroom teachers, students, parents, and administrators) to those school and community members who work with teachers or students or who have a vested interest in the outcome of mathematics education (e.g., school counselors, mathematics supervisors and staff developers, special education and/ or learning center teachers, counselors, and business people within the community). It is important to keep all of these groups of people in mind as you work to build support for your program.

One way to create support early on in the selection process is to hold discussions within the community about the district's goals for mathematics education. Use these discussions to review the NCTM *Standards,* your state curriculum frameworks, and any local standards or frameworks that are currently in use. Do they reflect your community's goals and expectations for mathematics education? What visions do you have of mathematics classrooms—what are students and teachers doing during lessons, what are children learning, and what do you want them to know and be able to do when they finish elementary, middle, and high school? These discussions will create a broad base of awareness among different stakeholder groups and provide opportunities to air disagreements or different perspectives. They also can be an important step toward building community commitment and enthusiasm for working with standards-based materials.

In this guide we assume that your community already has some set of standards for mathematics in place. You may have discussed and adopted your state frameworks, or used the NCTM *Standards* to develop a set of district standards of your own. If you have not, we strongly suggest that you undertake a series of conversations about setting standards as part of your "getting started" process. Even if your community already has a set of standards in place, you may want to hold some meetings to revisit them, making sure that they reflect your district's current goals and expectations. If you would like to learn more about setting district standards, a good resource is *Front-End Alignment*, a practical and informative guide.[3]

> *[The district] used community members all the way through the process of identifying what they wanted [the curriculum] to be, content-wise. They met late in the day so people could come. They talked together about what was important to look for in a curriculum—what they wanted students to know. They looked at the state content standards, doing some envisioning of what they wanted. (J.M., state associate director of curriculum)*

Identify and Support Teachers' Needs

Standards-based programs depend on teachers' active participation for successful implementation. A teacher's ability to manage classroom exploration and conversation, monitor students' work, and assess students' progress toward deeper understanding is central. These are often skills teachers have not been required to cultivate before. Identifying teachers' needs for support and developing appropriate responses to these needs are two key factors in the adoption process.

> *One thing that has been loud and clear at all grade levels: [the need for] staff development. I hear it over and over. If you adopt these curricula, you need ongoing staff development. Otherwise, you get folks going over to [an educational materials store], buying workbooks and using those. (K.V., mathematics curriculum specialist)*

---

[3] Mitchell, Ruth. (1996). *Front-End Alignment.* Washington, DC: The Education Trust.

PART II

The Curriculum Selection Process

Part II

The Curriculum Selection Process

Though the actual choice of a curriculum is, of course, the cornerstone of the process, this event is surrounded by a lot of other work, which we describe in this part of the guide. Some of this work is straightforward and logistical, for example, setting up a selection committee, creating access to materials under review, and recording evaluations of curricula. Other pieces require substantive work, for example, collecting information to characterize the district's current awareness and experience with standards-based mathematics materials, developing selection criteria for assessing curricula, planning for transitions across grades, and designing and evaluating a pilot phase.

Although it may seem premature to anticipate how you will implement a program before you even know which curricula you will be reviewing or as you are poring over materials that may never end up on bookshelves in your district, nonetheless, implementation is one of the most important issues to attend to during selection. Because both the content and the pedagogy of standards-based programs make new demands on teachers and students, you must make your selection with an eye toward the particular demands of each curriculum, and how those demands would be met in classrooms throughout your district. With standards-based curricula, selection and implementation issues are closely linked. It is for this reason that we speak of "selection and implementation" almost as if it were a single idea.

CHAPTER 3

Creating a Selection Committee

Your selection committee will allow you to share the work involved in choosing a mathematics curriculum and will help create links to the larger community during the adoption process. Traditionally, selection committees have met for a relatively short time to look through the newest editions of familiar curricula. When a district reviews standards-based programs for possible adoption, the work of the selection committee expands considerably. Committee members will have to examine candidate curricula in greater depth in order to become aware of important differences among the curricula's structure and organization, teacher support materials, treatment of mathematics, and pedagogical approaches. The committee will want to consider how likely the district is to welcome a new curriculum and how confident teachers will feel about implementing it. Committee members may also be called upon to be spokespeople for the selection process itself and for the choice to adopt an innovative, standards-based program. The committee, therefore, serves a variety of purposes:

- furnishing mathematical and instructional expertise for curriculum review itself

- promoting understanding about standards-based curricula

- building community trust and support

Factors to Consider When Assembling a Committee

There are two major factors to consider when you are putting together a selection committee. The first is its function: the role your committee will play in the selection process. The second is its composition: the groups that should be represented on the committee, the expertise that will help you to make a good selection, and the particular individuals who should serve as committee members. Both factors are described in more detail below.

Function of the Committee

The kind of committee you put together depends on the functions it will serve. In some districts the selection committee makes the curriculum selection decision, while in other districts the committee is advisory, serving as a curriculum study group. While it is common to use a committee to aid in the selection process, it is not universal. If your district has other mechanisms for fulfilling the functions generally served by a committee—e.g., sharing the work load, providing a forum for discussion of different curricula, representing various stakeholder groups, and making decisions—then you may decide against convening a formal committee at all. There is certainly no reason to create more committee work if you don't need to!

We do have a word of caution about the decision-making process in general. It is important to be clear at the outset about the kind of input you expect from committee members (or, if you don't have a formal committee, from people who want to participate in some aspect of the process) and about how their input will be used in reaching a decision about adoption. If everyone understands how the decision will be made and how their input will figure into it, you can avoid the possibility of later disagreements or disappointment about how the process played out.

Decision-making committees. In general, committees that make selection decisions tend to be smaller than advisory committees, as large groups often make the decision-making process unwieldy and inefficient. Committees may use different modes of reaching a decision: some rely on majority vote; others prefer to work toward consensus. Voting can be a relatively quick procedure, though it runs the risk of failing to build a strong commitment to any one curriculum. (Does a program that "wins" by a slim margin represent a clear mandate? How does the committee reconcile different preferences that may persist even after a vote is taken?) Reaching consensus can be time consuming, and sometimes it is very difficult to achieve. However, the advantage of reaching consensus is that it creates a sense of the leadership's unified commitment to and advocacy of the program selected.

Advisory committees. In some districts the selection committee serves an advisory capacity, helping the administration collect information and review potential curricula but not participating formally in the selection decision itself. Generally, advisory committees can be larger and more inclusive than decision-making ones. Because committee members do not make the selection decision, they need not be involved in all aspects of the process. Therefore, more people can participate, serving on subcommittees or working groups that report to the committee chair.

Advisory committees are common in districts where the committee chair wants the assistance and advice of a committee but also wants to maintain final control over the decision-making process. There are various reasons for wanting an advisory committee. Some districts may see no reason to change their history of making decisions this way, or they may view curriculum selection as an important and appropriate responsibility of the traditional decision maker (usually the mathematics coordinator or associate superintendent of curriculum and instruction). Other districts may choose to involve as many people as possible in the process in order to maximize buy-in, and still others may want to maintain control of the process to ensure that the curriculum selection furthers the district leadership's vision for mathematics education.

Composition of the Committee

As you think about committee membership, identify the kinds of expertise and experiences that will help you make your decision: Who possesses the mathematical knowledge you'll need to review program content? Who can help you assess the pedagogical approaches used by different curricula? Who can address the political issues you are likely to confront? Who can help you solicit feedback from different constituencies? Construct your committee to provide both the expertise you need to make a solid educational decision and the credibility to promote curriculum buy-in within the community.

Expertise

It is important to have people with different areas of expertise serve on your selection committee. A committee that represents diverse viewpoints and areas of expertise can offer a fuller, more balanced assessment of the different curricula. Classroom teachers, school counselors, teachers who serve students with limited English proficiency, K–12 mathematics coordinators, and special education teachers will each be sensitive to different aspects of the curriculum and will be able to provide feedback about the areas that they know best.

If you are selecting a curriculum at a single level (elementary, middle, or high school), you should include teachers from the other grade levels on your committee in order to help you think about cross-grades articulation (i.e., how the new curriculum will fit with the curricula for both the preceding and following grade levels). For example, an elementary teacher will have important input about the ways different middle school curricula will fit with the current elementary curriculum, and can provide a perspective on the mathematical skills and understanding that students leaving elementary school will bring to middle school mathematics. Conversely, a middle school teacher can provide perspectives on the mathematics that prospective elementary curricula must cover for students to be ready for the middle school program.

> *In the school system, we had the curriculum leaders (supervisors), at both the middle and high school levels and a few other school administrators [on the Advisory Board that reviewed curricula]. We had several teachers who were on the Advisory Board, and lots of parents who were academics or who worked as scientists or engineers, etc. (M.N., high school teacher leader)*

Special education or resource room teachers will be able to review materials with the particular learning needs of the students they serve in mind. As standards-based materials include more written text and require students to do more reading than has traditionally been the case in mathematics class, language arts teachers sometimes sit on adoption committees. Teachers who work with students with limited English proficiency or students whose home language is not English will also have valuable perspectives on the materials.

It is critical that you include people on your committee who are themselves experienced with mathematical investigation. It is much easier for those who have been mathematical enquirers themselves to understand the intent and vision of standards-based curricula. Committee members who are able to draw on their own experiences as learners can envision how different programs would (and would not) elicit such learning in students. It is also important to include people who are strong mathematically and can evaluate the content of the curricula.

Accountability and Buy-in

A diverse committee will ensure that different groups feel they have a voice in the process and can promote their sense of investment in the resulting selection. There is, however, a tension between representing different perspectives on the committee and putting together a group that shares enough of a viewpoint to be able to move forward on seriously considering a standards-based curriculum. We are not suggesting that you include people who are hostile to standards-based mathematics reform, but rather that you collect a group of people who will review the materials with a critical, yet sympathetic, eye. Nonetheless, this tension is very real, and each district must find a way to strike its own balance.

It is also a challenge to find a sensible way to involve other community members in the selection process. Parents and local employers can provide perspectives on practical expectations for a student's mathematics education and can ensure representation of these important constituencies within the community. Their participation can also help to build community buy-in for a standards-based adoption. However, sitting on a selection committee may not be the best use of their time; they may be able to convey their impressions effectively as occasional consultants, without having to sit through many afternoons or evenings of meetings. You should therefore think about how best to make use of community members' perspectives. One of the best ways to move forward on this issue is to talk with colleagues from other districts to learn from their experiences.

They made sure they involved community members, who represented a broad range of science employers in the area—a service manager for a local car dealer, an egg [carton] manufacturer, and [people] involved in natural resources. They also involved a lot of teachers. They didn't want anyone to be able to say, "It was that school's decision, not ours." (J.M., state associate director for curriculum)

Positioning the committee to encourage buy-in within district constituencies is a very important task. The more you can think strategically from the outset about ways to assemble a group of people who represent different stakeholders and will help advocate for standards-based programs, the greater your chances of a broad base of support for your adoption.

Getting Started as a Committee

The more diverse your committee, the more you need to begin your work together with some activities to orient the group to the goals and principles of standards-based mathematics education. Some districts create a half-day or full-day orientation to introduce committee members to the philosophy behind standards-based mathematics education and to establish some shared understanding about the meaning of terms commonly used by the reform movement (e.g., "hands-on learning," "mathematical inquiry"). As one mathematics coordinator observed, "People can use the same words and mean really different things. We needed some ways to develop congruence about what we were talking about." Begin the orientation with a discussion of the differences in both the mathematical content and the pedagogy of standards-based curricula. The following outline can help you plan such a discussion:

Differences in Mathematical Content

- There is a greater emphasis on mathematical thinking.

- The content is organized in terms of mathematical strands and important concepts.

- New content has been added.

- Topics may be taught at different grade levels than has traditionally been the case.

Differences in Pedagogical Approach

- Mathematical understanding, confidence, and interest are assumed to be attainable for *all* students.

- Students are actively involved in *doing* mathematics in cooperative groupings as well as individually, using a variety of materials.

- Mathematical discourse is a major component of standards-based classrooms.

- Technology and manipulatives are used as tools to reason about mathematical situations.

The facilitators for this orientation should be people whose own practices have been informed by the *Standards*. District mathematics supervisors and master teachers often make effective facilitators and presenters. Look for teachers who have been using standards-based materials and instructional techniques in their classrooms and who can also engage other adults in work that illustrates the philosophy and goals of standards-based mathematics education. If you don't have the resources within your own district to offer orientation sessions, see whether teacher educators from a local college or university could do the facilitation. Another way to provide orientation for your committee is to send a district team to the "Considering New Curricula" seminar offered by the K–12 Mathematics Curriculum Center (see Appendix 1 for contact information).

> Before ever seeing [curriculum] materials we spent two full days orienting the committee, bringing the committee up to speed on what to look for. We introduced the NCTM **Standards**, the state frameworks, talked about the reform effort in math. From my point of view we were trying to educate the folks. Many people in this day and age might be looking for drill and practice; we wanted to give them a broader perspective. We talked about manipulatives—found that people didn't know what these were, and so we learned that we had to clarify the terms, to be clear and not to use "education-ese." (V.M., supervisor of math, science, and technology)

Firsthand experience with standards-based mathematics learning is the best way to understand what it is all about. Have your committee do some mathematics themselves, working through a lesson from one of the new curricula. Working together on mathematics will provide a shared experience that can serve as a common reference point and can help members build a greater personal appreciation for the kind of mathematical learning and teaching promoted by standards-based curriculum and instruction. Start with mathematics problems everyone can understand so that all of your committee members will have a chance to engage with the mathematical ideas and see how they develop. (You also want to avoid creating unnecessary discomfort for anyone on the committee; working on mathematics in public can be a harrowing experience for people with little confidence in their own mathematical abilities. See the "DO" and "DON'T" lists for doing mathematics in public in Chapter 10, "Community Support.") Select problems that require both higher-order thinking and computational skills; your purpose is to provide people with an opportunity to engage in mathematical thinking, not to choose examples that will raise concerns about the balance between learning skills and concepts.

Another excellent way for your committee to gain firsthand experience with standards-based learning is to observe in classrooms. When committee members can see standards-based instruction in action, observing students and talking with teachers, they will have some concrete images of the kind of learning that standards-based programs seek to promote. This will help committee members imagine how the curricula they are reviewing might actually be used in their own district. Before going into classrooms, develop as a committee some shared perspectives for your observations.

Choosing Curricula to Review

Once the committee's orientation is completed, you will turn your attention more fully to the task of sorting through potential curricula for review. With so many products on the market, paring down choices to a manageable group can seem daunting. Reorganization within the publishing industry has not made the situation any easier, as a single company may now carry several curricula and it may be difficult to get a handle on what makes each of them unique. The following strategies and resources should help you sort your way through this initial phase of the selection process.

- **Talk with people in other districts about their adoption processes.** One of the best ways to get a sense of different curricula is to learn about other districts' experiences—getting an "in the trenches" perspective. Talk with friends and colleagues who have recently been involved in mathematics adoptions to find out which materials they considered, what they ended up selecting, what their reasons were, and how their implementation is faring.

- **Get recommendations from teachers in your district who have been active in mathematics education reform.** These teachers are among your best resources. They understand mathematics education reform, they have been using innovative materials in their own classrooms, and they're aware of your district's particular conditions and circumstances.

- **Go to state, regional, and national NCTM conferences.** These meetings are one of the few places where many different curricula are available at the same time. Use the meetings to attend sessions about standards-based curricula, look through different curricula at the exhibit hall, talk with publishers' representatives about their materials, and find other meeting participants who can share their experiences and opinions.

- **Contact publishers for catalogues, sample materials, and initial sales presentations.** These will give you a sense of the variety of curricula that are available and some cursory ideas of the materials themselves.

- **Contact the NSF-funded implementation centers and their satellites.** The K–12 Mathematics Curriculum Center has brief curriculum summaries for all 13 comprehensive curricula supported by the Center. *Curriculum Perspectives* offer more detailed information about the curricula, based on practitioners' accounts of their experiences.[4] You can also contact the grade-level implementation centers and their satellites for information about seminars, workshops, and print resources about specific curricula. (Contact information is listed in Appendices 1 and 2.)

---

[4] *Curriculum Perspectives* will be available in Spring 1999 from the K–12 Mathematics Curriculum Center.

CHAPTER 4

Taking Stock: Assessing Current Resources and Future Needs

Districts begin looking for a new curriculum because they believe that their present program is lacking in one way or another. Perhaps teachers are dissatisfied with the current curriculum, or the state has adopted a new open-ended assessment that isn't a good match with the current program. These kinds of catalysts can provide powerful energy and focus to your process. You can use them as touchstones, checking each curriculum against your central issues to see how well it addresses them. These issues can also be used to gauge your implementation needs and identify resources for meeting them.

In contemplating a new kind of mathematics curriculum, you are asking people in a variety of roles to anticipate changing their work and their ideas about mathematics education. Your review process should include some form of needs and resources assessment to help you determine more specifically the kinds of changes people will need to make, and the support they will need. This assessment will give you an accurate reading of current district policy and practice, an idea of which changes will work in your district, a projection of your future needs, and a sense of the resources you can enlist (or need to find) to move toward your vision for mathematics education.

You may decide to undertake a formal assessment process, collecting information through focus groups, questionnaires, school visits, or other means.[5] Alternatively, you may decide to forgo organized data collection in favor of a more informal approach. The decision about the rigor of your assessment process depends on a number of factors, for example, the size and diversity of your district, the time and staff available for this task, and the existing districtwide mechanisms for communicating about needs and resources.

Such an assessment serves several purposes. It will help you develop criteria for evaluating curricula during your selection phase. For instance, if a catalyst for your adoption is the need to prepare students for state-mandated tests that use open-ended problems and rubric scoring, you know that you will need to review curricula with this goal in mind. Your needs assessment will also help you gauge the current interest and readiness within the district for adopting standards-based materials. This information is particularly important for anticipating those aspects of the implementation that will need particular attention and support.

---

[5] If your district is considering applying to the National Science Foundation for a Local Systemic Change (LSC) grant, your application will include a needs assessment.

To begin your assessment, you should do the following:

- **Revisit past experiences.** To move toward your goal, you must know from where you are starting. Ask yourselves these questions:

    - What aspects of our current mathematics program have been working well?

    - What would we like to change, and why?

- **Anticipate future needs.** One of your biggest assets is the ability to think critically about your district's strengths and weaknesses. Collect information from your own district and talk with colleagues in other districts about their implementation experiences. Ask yourselves these questions:

    - What professional development and other district support will teachers need to implement standards-based curricula?

    - What do district leaders need to know and be able to do to ensure successful implementation?

    - What support will students need to succeed with the new curriculum?

    - What can we do to help parents accept and support the curriculum?

    - What other challenges can we expect during selection and implementation?

Gathering Information about Your Needs and Resources

You can use the information you gather to think strategically about the resources you will need to support a successful adoption. The following sections describe broad categories of needs and resources to consider. The chapter concludes with a list of sample questions for your needs and resources assessment.

Current Mathematics Programs

Some districts are motivated to consider new mathematics curricula because dissatisfied teachers leave their books in the storeroom and search out other materials for their lessons. As you plan for your next selection, think about what you *do* like about your current program and also what you would like to change about it. For example, your current curriculum may do an excellent job of introducing the notion of a function or developing the relationship between decimals and fractions, and you will want to make sure that the next curriculum you choose does the same. Alternatively, you may think that your current program does an inadequate job of motivating mathematical ideas, and you want your next curriculum to offer more active exploration of ideas, framing them in engaging contexts. When you have a clear idea of the strengths and limitations of your current program, you can focus on redressing the limitations as you review potential replacements.

District Leadership

District leadership is critical to creating a coherent and successful mathematics program. Administrators—the associate superintendent of curriculum and instruction, mathematics coordinators and principals, the special education director, and the district superintendent— play central roles in selecting and implementing standards-based curricula. Their authority is necessary to maintain a steady course toward district goals and support teachers' implementation efforts. Those with mathematical and instructional expertise serve as resources to teachers, and the entire leadership team can act as advocates and spokespeople

Leadership is the key. People can do things on their own, but [their efforts] won't be sustained unless there's a unified approach mandated within the district. (G.T., middle school teacher leader)

to the community, taking a "big picture" perspective on reform and coordinating efforts across subject areas and between grades. Effective administrators are able to rally support for improving mathematics education, troubleshooting and running interference if problems arise.

Because many administrators lack firsthand classroom experience with standards-based mathematics teaching, they may be more familiar with the rhetoric of reform than they are with the specific rewards and challenges of running an effective standards-based classroom. It is important for district leaders to see such classrooms in action and to recognize effective instruction and learning. As one middle school teacher noted, "It takes collaboration and leadership to make sure that teachers learn about what's behind the trappings of reform." The administration must understand the spirit as well as the "trappings" of standards-based mathematics curricula and must help ensure that teachers focus on developing students' mathematical understanding, not simply on introducing new classroom structures and techniques, such as cooperative group work, use of manipulatives, multi-day lessons, and journal writing. This may require orientation and professional development for administrators.

Teacher leaders are another critical component of district leadership. They are generally at the forefront of the teaching force, experimenting with new curricula and making new forms of instruction a reality in their classrooms. As known and trusted leaders in the teaching community, they will be

Pick a well-known and well-respected person to lead the charge. Many people will follow, based on the reputation of a key leader. (M.N., high school teacher leader)

able to speak convincingly and authoritatively to teacher colleagues, administrators, and parents alike. They can serve as mentors for other teachers in the district, speak from experience about the benefits and difficulties of using new materials, and act as advocates for standards-based mathematics education with the administration, colleagues, and the larger community.

When you are taking stock of your district leadership you should not forget those individuals who serve as liaisons with the larger community, but make sure that they have had some orientation to the ideas behind mathematics education reform. For example, since parents may bring questions and concerns to the school board, it is important that board members understand the goals and values of standards-based mathematics education, and are able to speak to them. If possible, take community liaisons to visit classrooms using standards-based programs to give them a sense of the kind of teaching and learning these curricula are seeking to promote.

Teachers' Readiness

Ultimately, the success of a curriculum lies in the work that teachers and students do together in the classroom each day. Because a teacher's commitment to the principles and methods of a curriculum is a major part of the equation, it is important to know about teachers' readiness to use standards-based curricula. These programs may challenge teachers in a number of ways. You will want to find out how prepared teachers feel they are to implement a standards-based program in terms of the following:

- mathematical content

- pedagogical approaches

- assessment strategies

- classroom management

- personal interest and investment in using new curricula

> *The key is being able to translate [the underlying philosophy of standards-based reform] to the teacher who has been through waves of reform many times. Many are skeptical and have a "show me" attitude. (J.G., assistant superintendent for curriculum and instruction)*

The information you collect can help you determine the kind of professional development and support that teachers will need to implement successfully the curriculum you choose. It can also help you think about how to approach teachers who are resistant to or uninterested in using standards-based programs.

You will need to know about the kinds of resources you have, or will need, in order to plan effective professional development support for your teachers. Publishers and community, business, and university partners are among the resources you can call on to help you plan and deliver professional development.

Parents' Opinions and Concerns

Many of today's parents learned mathematics by rote and without much of a sense of *why* all those rules they learned work out as they do. Some parents may see standards-based mathematics curricula as insufficiently rigorous to be effective learning tools. Others may see these curricula as a welcome effort to make mathematics more comprehensible. Learning how parents are thinking about their children's mathematics education will help you plan ways to encourage parental buy-in and participation in their children's mathematics learning.

Additional Considerations: District Policies and Student Attitudes

Other factors may also influence your selection and implementation, although they are less likely to have a major effect on shaping your adoption process. One of these factors is district policy. Be aware that some policies may support adoption of standards-based curricula (for example, block scheduling allows for longer class periods; generous professional development policies can contribute to teachers' comfort and confidence during implementation), while others may pose barriers. (For example, union injunctions against accepting additional work responsibilities may make it difficult for teachers to assume informal leadership roles; difficulties in scheduling common preparation times may make it harder for teachers to work together on implementation).

Students' attitudes toward mathematics, their feelings about their current mathematics experiences, and their familiarity with different instructional techniques may also influence implementation. Students who have already had some exposure to standards-based materials will have developed working styles and habits of mind that they will be able to use with the new curricula. Those who are accustomed to a more traditional style of instruction may find the expectations of a reform-based program foreign and even somewhat uncomfortable. Just as you will need to gauge teachers' readiness for adopting a standards-based pedagogy, you will need to think about how adopting a standards-based curriculum will challenge your students in terms of participating in (and learning from) class discussions, working collaboratively, and reading and writing.

Methods for Gathering Information

There are different ways to collect information about district needs and resources. You could take an informal approach, relying on your committee's collective knowledge of the district to make your assessments. Using this approach takes little time but may fail to identify the full range of needs or resources within the district. Although it requires more time, taking a more systematic approach to collecting information will provide you with a more accurate picture of the conditions within your district. There are several ways to collect formal information about district needs:

- **Surveys.** Surveys are particularly good for collecting a lot of information fairly quickly. They don't allow you to collect a lot of detail, but they can be a good place to start. For example, you can use a survey to find out how many teachers are aware of the NCTM *Standards* and/or the state framework, have supplemented textbook lessons with "hands-on" activities, or have been involved in professional development for mathematics education. (However, a survey won't tell you about the quality of the activities teachers are using or the changes in practice they have made as a result of their professional development. Survey results may help you identify issues or questions requiring follow-up.)

Summarize the survey information you collect in tallies or tables to help you see patterns in people's responses.

When you send out written surveys, you run the risk that people will not return them. You can increase the chances of returns (and therefore of an accurate assessment of the whole group you are surveying) by having people fill out surveys on the spot (for example, at the end of a meeting) or by doing them over the phone.

- **Meetings and focus groups.** You can use meetings with teachers, administrators, and community members to brainstorm resources and learn about needs. If you have conducted surveys and have questions about some of the results, meetings can help to clarify these. These meetings are also often good opportunities to hear different perspectives. Review your notes of meetings and organize the information into categories such as teacher support, budget, assessment, and community education to help you interpret your data about needs and resources.

- **Classroom observation.** Observing in classrooms will give you a firsthand sense of mathematics instruction in the district, supplementing other information you collect. If you decide to visit classrooms as part of your needs/resources assessment, make sure that you see both teachers who are working toward mathematics education reform and teachers who are not. It's important to know what typical classrooms are like in your district and what kinds of teacher leadership are available.

- **Selected interviews.** Interviewing key people can help you learn a lot about a particular issue or subject without doing extra legwork. Rather than visiting many classrooms in the district, for example, you could talk with the district's mathematics supervisor, mathematics department head, or principals about what mathematics instruction is generally like in the district. Prepare guiding questions or topics to ensure that the conversation will stay on track, and that you will learn about the things you need to know. Take written notes during your interview so that you can review them later, categorize responses, and make a chart or table to display the information you have analyzed.

Summary

Although it may seem somewhat counterintuitive, a successful selection process rests largely on thinking about implementation. Your adoption will stand or fall as much on the way that the district *uses* the new materials as it will on the particular activities that comprise lessons, or the organization of the materials themselves. Because of this, it is important to spend time during the selection phase anticipating the general kinds of implementation needs you will face, evaluating your current resources, and planning ways to access others. Conducting a needs and resources assessment will help you make informed decisions about curriculum selection and implementation.

Be strategic about the kinds of information you collect; the point is to *help* you make decisions, not to inundate you with additional tasks. It can be a lot easier to gather information than to make sense of it, so think through what you need to know and how you can learn about it. Plan to spend time analyzing your data. Summarize your findings in tables, charts, or tallies that will help you see patterns, and then use your data to guide the questions you ask during the selection phase and the plans you make for implementation.

Sample Questions: Needs and Resources Assessment

This section contains sample questions for a needs and resources assessment. In general, the questions are aimed at collecting the following three kinds of information:

- the current state of affairs in your district

- the kind of mathematics education for which you are aiming

- the resources you have and those you will need to achieve your goals

The questions are organized into two main categories:

- Current Mathematics Program

- District Readiness

There are more questions offered here than you could reasonably use in any one assessment. Our purpose is to take a comprehensive look at the issues that can influence selection and implementation of standards-based curricula rather than to present a protocol that you can copy and use at your next opportunity. Instead, take these questions as a starting point for creating an assessment that focuses on the key issues for your own district.

Current Mathematics Program

Mathematical Content

- What important areas of mathematics does your current program address well?

- What mathematical areas would you like to see more strongly addressed in your next program?

- How does your current program meet state and national tests?

- What are the strengths/weaknesses of your current curriculum for diverse groups of students (e.g., limited English proficiency, special education, bilingual, gifted and talented)?

- How have past efforts to introduce new mathematics curricula fared in your district? What can you learn from past experiences?

Curriculum

- What aspects of the current curriculum do teachers feel are effective for promoting student learning?

- How are teachers using the current curricula? Do they use them pretty much as they come, or are they making major modifications or additions to the materials?

- What kind of instructional materials would teachers like to be using?

Students

- How satisfied are you with your students' current mathematics learning/performance?

- What are the biggest challenges for your students in learning mathematics?

- How well does your current mathematics curriculum meet the range of students' learning needs within your district?

- How engaged are students with their study of mathematics?

Cross-Grades Articulation

- How well do your current programs fit together? In other words, how well does the elementary program prepare students for the middle school curriculum, or the middle school program prepare students for the high school curriculum?

District Readiness

Leadership

- What kind of support for mathematics education reform do you get from the following groups or individuals?

    - superintendent

    - mathematics supervisors/department heads

    - teacher leaders

    - school board

- What new challenges will be created for leaders with the adoption of a standards-based mathematics curriculum? Can our current leaders respond to them?

Teachers

- How do teachers in your district currently incorporate the following instructional techniques into their mathematics lessons?

    - classroom discussion

    - open-ended questioning

    - cooperative groupings

    - multiple representations of problem solutions

    - drill and practice for facts and algorithms

    - standard and alternative assessment strategies

    - writing

    - manipulatives

    - technology (calculators and/or computers)

- How receptive are teachers to adoption of a standards-based curriculum? What are their fears or concerns?

- Will your teachers need professional development in any of the following areas?

  - mathematics content

  - pedagogy

  - classroom management

- What are your professional development resources (e.g., money, lead teachers, staff developers, outside consultants)?

- What is your current strategy for providing mathematics professional development? How successful is it?

Parents

- What do parents want their children to learn about mathematics in elementary school, middle school, and high school?

- What satisfies parents about the current mathematics program?

- What are parents' concerns about their children's current mathematics education?

- What are their concerns about changing to a new mathematics curriculum?

- What opportunities for learning about mathematics education in the district do parents currently have (e.g., math nights, print resources, short seminars)?

CHAPTER 5

Planning for Cross-Grades Transitions

Ideally, your mathematics program would take a coherent approach to mathematical content and pedagogy from the first day of kindergarten through high school graduation. In reality this may be a difficult goal to achieve, particularly if your district is in the process of aligning curriculum and instruction with your state frameworks and the NCTM *Standards*. It is important for you to understand how your curricula at the different grade spans (elementary, middle, and high school) fit together, both in terms of content and instructional style, and to anticipate ways to deal with places where the fit is problematic. For example, you will need to know whether there are certain grades where students experience a significant shift in the work they're expected to do, or grades where teachers feel that students enter without requisite knowledge or skills.

Districts that have recently adopted standards-based curricula report that students must make the greatest adjustment as they shift from more traditional to more innovative materials (or, occasionally, from innovative materials back to traditional ones). These shifts often coincide with students' moves from one grade span to another: from elementary to middle school, middle to high school, or high school to college. (These transition points often involve a larger pattern of change, which includes moving from one school building to another and adjusting to new school structures, class schedules, and teacher expectations.) It's particularly important for you to identify the points of fit and mismatch between the two curricula so you can help students accomplish these transitions as smoothly as possible.

> In eighth grade kids do group work, use calculators and other manipulatives, and have discussion in class. In ninth grade instruction is in the form of teacher presentation and working problems in the textbook. Some teachers discourage use of calculators, and student assessment is based only on tests. It's a huge change and, frankly, I don't know how the kids do it. (G.T., middle school teacher)

The two most commonly raised issues of concern are students' preparation (Are students developing the skills and understanding they need to learn mathematics at the next level?) and continuity of instruction (Are the curricula we are using at the different grades based on common goals and strategies for student learning?). You will need to consider these questions whether you are choosing a program for a single grade span or adopting standards-based curricula across the board.

If you are adopting standards-based curricula across the K–12 grade span, you may have assumed that all standards-based curricula will articulate well with one another and that taking a K–12 approach will obviate the need to ask how programs at different grade levels fit together. Unfortunately, this is not entirely the case. Standards-based curricula do share some family resemblances because they were developed from a common set of underlying principles about mathematics, mathematics learning, and mathematics teaching. However, there are also variations in both content and pedagogy. Because the various curricula were not developed with the primary goal of connecting smoothly to curricula at other grade spans to form comprehensive K–12 packages, you will need to consider issues of articulation as you make your selection. While you obviously need to focus most intensely on the characteristics of candidate curricula at the particular grade span you are selecting, also look forward and backward to see how each candidate would fit with your overall plan for K–12 mathematics. In particular, keep an eye open for the following key transition issues, which center around changes in how students and teachers experience pedagogical and mathematical aspects of the curriculum across grades K–12.

Pedagogy

Your district may be planning to adopt new curricula across grades K–12 or you may be focusing your present adoption at one of the three grade spans: elementary, middle, or high school. In either case, it is important to know how the instructional approaches align across grades K–12. For example, will expectations for students to communicate their mathematical ideas in writing and through discussion be consistent across grades, or will students have to adjust to shifts from heavy emphasis on communication of mathematical thinking in some grades to relatively little emphasis in others? Students whose earlier experience centered on lectures and individual seatwork will need some time to adjust to classroom lessons that are heavily based in discourse. In contrast, students who have been learning mathematics through exploration and discussion and then move to a curriculum that takes a less interactive and inquiry-based approach will also need time to adjust. In either case, students may be confused and uncertain about the expectations for their work in class. It is important to know whether students will experience discontinuities in instructional approach when they move from one curriculum to another and to have a plan in place for responding to these discontinuities.

> *Right now, the greatest change is in fifth grade because of the reading and writing required in the new program. Kids are expected to read, to do a lot of self-teaching and investigation, and to respond to questions that are much more varied and thought-provoking than you would find in a traditional text-book. (L.U., K–8 mathematics coordinator)*

> *One program is more open-ended than the other. Using multiple strategies is really encouraged in our middle school program, [but] I would say in the high school curriculum, there is really one strategy that works for solving the problem. (J.F., K–12 mathematics supervisor)*

Mathematics Content

Overlaps or Gaps

You will need to look for possible overlaps and gaps in the content addressed at different grades, whether you are considering adoption of a standards-based curriculum at a single grade span or across all grades from kindergarten through grade 12. Although all the programs at an individual grade span work with the same fundamental ideas, they do vary in the ways they develop these ideas and, to an extent, in the points at which the ideas appear. An issue that one curriculum may introduce in seventh grade, for example, may be part of the sixth grade curriculum for another, or an idea that appears at the end of one of the elementary curricula may be introduced at the beginning of a middle school curriculum.

There's a good chance that you'll find overlaps (e.g., ideas introduced toward the end of one curriculum are also introduced at the beginning of another) or gaps (e.g., the curriculum you're using at the higher grade levels presumes that students have been introduced to ideas that were not sufficiently treated in the earlier curriculum) at the junctures between grade spans. These don't constitute cause for rejecting certain curricula, but you do need to be aware of possible gaps and overlaps in order to make adjustments. In general, you're most likely to find overlaps and gaps as you move from one curriculum to another, since the individual curricula strive for internal consistency and coherence. Therefore, pay particular attention to the boundaries between grade spans (around the fifth or sixth grade and again around eighth or ninth grade). You should also be alert to the possible gaps your high school students will experience in college courses and plan on adjusting your mathematics program accordingly.

Integrated Content

The issue of overlaps and gaps in curricula is a programmatic one, concerning the fit between your elementary, middle, and high school curricula. A version of this issue will play out at the individual student level as well, in the case of students who may move in and out of standards-based curricula within a single grade span.

As we used these programs, we found a huge overlap at the eighth and ninth grade between [our middle grades curriculum] and [our high school curriculum]. For the [less able] students, it's good for them to see the algebra content again in ninth grade, but for the [students who learn more quickly], I've heard that they're getting bored, and it's becoming an issue for parents. Students get lots of experience with linear, exponential, and quadratic relationships. [Our middle school program] is strong in those aspects of algebra, and the [high school] approach isn't different enough from that. The high school curriculum assumes that kids are coming from a traditional mathematics program. (J.F., K–12 mathematics coordinator)

Because the developers of standards-based curricula have taken a more integrated approach to mathematics content, interweaving content strands throughout the curriculum and developing ideas across grade spans, the content covered in individual grades may not correspond entirely to the topics covered in other mathematics curricula. This approach is characteristic of standards-based curricula at all grade levels, but it represents the most radical departure from the traditional organization of high school courses.

While this difference in approaches presents little difficulty when students are able to complete the entire curriculum, it may become problematic when students transfer in or out somewhere in the middle. You will need to anticipate the difficulties students will have either entering a standards-based curriculum or moving to a more traditional program. This is particularly important for high schools that offer both standards-based and traditional mathematics programs. It is important to know how to help students make the transition between the integrated approaches of standards-based high school curricula and the traditional Algebra I–Geometry–Algebra II–Trigonometry/PreCalculus sequence.

Grouping

As students make the transition from elementary school to the higher grades you may find that grouping and tracking issues emerge, despite the fact that standards-based curricula are designed for students of varying ability levels. Some districts have found they need to continue offering tracking options and accelerated courses in order to provide appropriate alternatives for students with different needs. We see this happening most often in an effort to provide students with access to algebra in the middle school and to Advanced Placement calculus in high school. Some districts use standards-based curricula for all of their middle and high school mathematics classes, but many find they need to offer additional options to students (and their parents). In some cases, districts have addressed this dilemma by offering students the choice of enrolling either in standards-based programs or in classes specifically geared toward the AP calculus track. In other districts, teachers have supplemented a standards-based curriculum to prepare students for more advanced course work.

Paying Attention to Cross-Grades Articulation

When you are in the throes of deciding which curriculum to adopt for a particular grade span, your focus is understandably directed at questions about the mathematics education your students will be receiving *at those grades*. However, it's also important to continue to keep articulation issues in mind as you make your choices so that you don't lose sight of the big picture. Below is some advice from others who have recently been through the adoption process.

Take a K-12 Perspective

Even if you're currently adopting a new curriculum at only one grade span, look at it in the context of its fit into the overall picture of your K–12 program. Taking a K–12 perspective doesn't necessarily mean that you need to have in place a 13-year sequence that is completely consistent in its approaches to content and pedagogy, but it does mean that you should be aware of potential discontinuities and have ideas for ways to maximize the coherence of students' mathematics education experience from kindergarten through their last high school mathematics course.

Collect Information about the Transition Points

Only a few districts have used standards-based curricula long enough to collect hard data about cross-grades articulation issues. For the time being, taking a K–12 perspective has largely been a matter of faith and speculation—we know relatively little about the particulars of what makes a transition between curricula rocky or smooth. However, both faith and skepticism can interfere with making informed decisions about implementation; what you need is real information. Talk with others about their experiences and plan to use your own implementation process to collect information about the articulation issues that emerge. This will not only help your own district address the issues more systematically and effectively, but it will provide data to other districts, which they can use to anticipate potential issues and plan appropriate interventions.

We're just starting to have that: significant numbers of students coming into the high school that experienced a significant amount of the new K–8 program and who have been through all of the programs. We didn't have good information about what was happening to kids. We didn't think about the transition issues as much as maybe we should have. (M.D., K–12 district mathematics supervisor)

Seek Perspectives from Others

Many districts across the country have shifted to using standards-based curricula or are currently in the process of doing so, and they can be a source of information about potential articulation issues. Publishers, curriculum developers, and especially other teachers, schools, and districts that have used these materials can be invaluable resources. They have experience with a variety of different models for articulation between programs, and you can learn from their successes as well as their mistakes.

Encourage Communication across Grade Levels

It is extremely important that teachers using new materials be able to establish effective lines of communication across the grade levels. Teachers will have questions for their colleagues in the lower grades about what incoming students already know and are able to do—especially if students' prior mathematics experiences are significantly different than in the past. Likewise, teachers need opportunities to communicate their assessment of their students' abilities and understanding to their colleagues in the upper grades. One concrete mechanism for ensuring such communication is to include on your selection committee teachers from grades that bracket the particular grade span under adoption, as has been previously suggested.

Consider Teacher Readiness and Support

Teachers' readiness to use new materials will influence your strategy for addressing articulation and transition issues. Even though it's desirable to have a consistent approach to mathematics learning from grade to grade, you won't gain anything in the long run by introducing new curricula in every grade before teachers are prepared to make good use of them. It's more important to ensure that you have the appropriate professional development and teacher support in place to help teachers make an effective transition to a new curriculum than it is to ensure that the curriculum materials are consistent from grade to grade.

CHAPTER 6

Developing and Applying Selection Criteria

When you design criteria to reflect your goals and address your needs, you will have a powerful tool to use in your selection process. Your criteria will standardize the ways committee members review candidate curricula and will focus your evaluation on how each curriculum would help you achieve your goals. The criteria provide a set of common questions to ask of each program. You can use these questions to compare different curricula and also to compare different reviewers' evaluations of the same materials. Much of the work you have already done to articulate your goals and assess community needs and resources will be useful in designing your selection criteria. Developing your selection criteria will also help you to continue clarifying and articulating your goals and values for mathematics education.

Begin working on your criteria early in the process to make sure you develop and refine a set of questions that address the issues that are most important to you. You should have a working set of criteria early enough so that you can practice using them before you begin reviewing curricula in earnest. This gives you time to calibrate the ways that people are using the criteria, see how long it takes to use the criteria to review a curriculum, and clear up any questions or problems that arise—similar to playing an open practice hand when you learn a new card game.

Don't skimp on developing your criteria—they will help make your selection process rigorous and thoughtful. It takes time and thought to construct them, but you don't have to start from scratch. There are a number of resources you can call on. Your state or local frameworks can serve as a touchstone for developing questions about *how* the curricula address these frameworks. (However, recognize that the wording in the frameworks themselves generally doesn't translate into good criteria because it usually lacks the necessary level of specificity.) With your frameworks (or the NCTM *Standards*) in mind, look at the review criteria you have used in the past and see which are still relevant. If you find that previous criteria fail to address your current goals, look elsewhere for guidance, for example, to colleagues in districts that have already explored standards-based curricula. We have included sample questions at the end of this chapter to get you started, and some additional examples used by districts are included in Appendix 4.

This chapter discusses some of the important issues to consider when crafting selection criteria, grouped into the following categories:

- mathematical content

- approaches to teaching

- approaches to learning

- presentation and organization of curriculum materials

The chapter concludes with a section on the design and use of selection criteria.

Mathematical Content

Because the mathematical content in standards-based programs is often not as apparent on brief examination as it is in traditional texts, you will have to study standards-based lessons more carefully to get their mathematical point(s). There are a number of reasons for this.

1. Units or chapters in standards-based programs may not be identified by topic, so you will have to look more closely to find out what mathematical ideas they address. Chapter titles may describe the contexts in which the mathematical ideas are presented rather than naming the ideas themselves—for example, "Family Portraits" focuses on comparing function families and "Between Never and Always" is a unit on probability. Many publishers do provide analyses of the curricula that identify the units addressing particular standards to help orient you to the mathematical content.

2. Standards-based curricula are more likely to integrate a number of different mathematical ideas within a single unit, resulting in a lack of strict correspondence between lesson and topic. Lessons that are, on the surface, about such practical problems as designing a house or planning a journey may contain opportunities to develop and practice a variety of skills and concepts, such as computing fractions, converting units of measurement, and writing and solving algebraic expressions. Because many standards-based curricula embed a good deal of problem solving and skill mastery in games or practical applications, you have to study lessons more carefully to make sure you don't overlook some of their mathematical goals.

3. Because lessons may extend over several days (or even weeks), the mathematical ideas they target unfold over time as well, which makes it difficult to review a single lesson and draw reliable conclusions about the mathematics being developed.

4. When programs embed mastery of technical skills in games or activities (a common feature of standards-based programs), reviewers may be inclined to conclude, incorrectly, that the curriculum does not provide opportunities for students to learn important facts and procedures.

In keeping with the recommendations of the *Standards,* some of the mathematical content also differs from that of traditional texts. The curricula include new content areas (e.g., discrete mathematics, probability, and data analysis) and focus less on procedural or computational topics (e.g., long division, factoring polynomials). You may find that topics and ideas traditionally taught at one grade level are introduced in a different grade, so you will have to keep an eye out for the progression of mathematical ideas. This is particularly true for the high school curricula, where integrated programs follow a pathway that differs from the traditional Algebra I–Geometry–Algebra II–Trigonometry/PreCalculus sequence.

As you examine different materials, take the time to look carefully at several of the units at each of the different grades. Work through a few of them yourselves to get a more concrete idea of how mathematical ideas and skills are developed within the lessons, and where these ideas might lead. Read the teacher's guide to see how the developers have framed the lesson: how clearly are the mathematical ideas that underlie it presented, and are these ideas important ones for students to learn? Check to see whether the teacher's guide offers samples of student work for the lesson. If there are samples, ask whether they will help teachers to anticipate the kinds of ideas they will encounter with their own students; if there aren't samples, look for other ways that the guide helps prepare teachers to promote students' mathematical thinking.

There are also important differences among the standards-based curricula. Though they all extend more active roles to students, they don't do this in the same ways, nor do they make the same pedagogical demands on teachers. The curricula also differ in the ways they motivate the mathematics itself: some focus directly on investigations of mathematical concepts and ways of thinking; some develop the mathematics through practical applications; some take a technological perspective; and some embed the mathematics in games, stories, or dilemmas. Since these differences can affect both the way that the curricula develop mathematical ideas and the ways that students learn them, you should examine curricula with an eye toward the approach that best suits your needs.

Approaches to Teaching

Standards-based curricula offer an important and challenging role for teachers. Teachers serve as brokers of the curriculum, providing the link between the written materials and the student. Since so much of the learning occurs through the particular interactions students have with the activities, their classmates, and their teachers, the curricula require teachers to make many complex judgments about moving students' learning forward. Teachers new to standards-based instruction may find it initially difficult to anticipate how students will respond to activities, or how the mathematical ideas in lessons will unfold. It is therefore important that standards-based curricula offer teachers guidance and support for transforming the written lesson into actual classroom work. As you review materials, pay particular attention to the quality of the teacher support materials for the different curricula.

There are particular elements of standards-based instruction that may be new and unfamiliar to teachers—for example, the emphasis on engaging students in mathematical processes, or asking them to explain and justify their answers to problems. Below, we identify some of the elements of standards-based instruction that you should consider when reviewing curricula.

Classroom Communication

The *Standards* emphasize classroom discourse as a driving force in the development of mathematical thinking and communication. As the focus of instruction shifts toward students' ability to reason about mathematics and justify their ideas, students' presentation and discussion of their ideas takes a more central place in the classroom. Your selection criteria should include questions about how different programs encourage and support teachers in establishing mathematical conversations in class. The criteria should also include questions about how the materials support teachers in evaluating the mathematical validity of students' responses and asking questions that promote further learning.

Use of Manipulatives and Technology (Calculators and Computers)

Mathematics curricula are no longer distinguished by *whether* they use manipulatives or technology. Many programs—standards-based and more traditional ones alike—now include lessons that involve concrete materials such as base 10 blocks, Cuisenaire rods, counters, fraction pieces, pattern blocks, geoboards, and algebra tiles. Calculators are also commonly recommended for some activities. Certain mathematics programs also use computers, though with the advent of relatively inexpensive graphing calculators, computers are not as central to many curricula as they were expected to be even just a few years ago.

As you review curricula, think about how manipulatives and technology are used and how the *way* they are used reflects your district's agenda for students' mathematical learning. Notice whether the curriculum offers students the opportunity to use calculators as tools and resources for reasoning mathematically. Also consider when calculators or computers function as computation tools and when they offer ways for students to learn skills and represent and model mathematical concepts.

Once you have considered the roles played by manipulatives and technology in a given curriculum, you must ask whether this role is consistent with your expectations and how the curriculum helps teachers make effective use of these materials. For example, does the curriculum offer practical advice about setting up the classroom and organizing students' access to manipulatives, calculators, and computers? What guidance does the curriculum offer teachers for using these tools effectively for instruction?

Assessment

You'll probably attend to issues of assessment much more during the implementation phase, but it's also important to consider how assessments are structured within the various curricula as you are making your selection. This will help you see how different curricula align with district perspectives on assessment. As you review materials you should think about how they handle two different types of assessment: those that help guide classroom instruction and those that evaluate student progress.

Classroom assessments that inform instruction help teachers focus on what students do and don't understand, while there is still time to help them understand more. Opportunities for ongoing classroom assessment occur in the course of regular class work and discussion. To some extent, this is the role that homework, tests, and quizzes have traditionally played. As the focus has turned more and more toward how students think about their work and not just whether they are getting the right answers, classroom assessments now focus on helping teachers more fully understand their students' thinking, so they can plan instruction to move that thinking forward. As you review curricula, look for the ways that each program helps teachers focus on their students' thinking through classroom-based assessments.

Assessments that are evaluative (for example, end-of-unit tests, midterms and finals, and state and national tests) are important for documenting student learning and progress. They provide an accounting of the degree of students' success in mathematics classes and are used as a way of ensuring the district's accountability to students and parents. You will need to be clear about the kind of mathematical competence you want (or need) to assess, and review curricula with an eye toward the match between your mathematical goals for students and the mathematical focus of the materials. This is a question you will ask when you are reviewing curricula for their content; you can ask it again with an "assessment spin" to it: Will the curriculum help students develop the understanding, skills, and attitudes they need to do well on the tests they must take to advance to higher levels of education? (This is often a particularly important question for parents.)

One salient issue is the degree to which assessments (particularly such high-stakes tests as college boards and state competency exams) are aligned with the curricula. A common concern is that standards-based curricula won't fully prepare students for standardized tests. In fact, there is little research data about this issue, and no clear support for this concern: there are many anecdotal reports of district scores on standardized tests holding steady or improving, and also some reports of temporary drops in computational scores that may well be due to difficulties with implementation. As with any new adoption, there may be a temporary drop in scores as teachers are learning to fully implement the new curriculum. Ask publishers and the NSF-funded implementation centers for imple- mentation data they have collected and talk with other

Because [the program we chose] doesn't align with MATs [our current assessment instrument], I asked the board of education to hold off on looking there for results, because they wouldn't show right away. (C.U., associate superintendent of curriculum and instruction)

districts that have used the curricula you are considering to find out how their students are performing.

For these reasons, it is very important that you carefully consider how adopting a standards-based program will align with current district and state assessment policies. If you anticipate a mismatch between curriculum objectives and the critical assessment measures to which you are held accountable, you will need to develop a plan to address the lack of alignment between teaching and testing. For example, you can include supplementary materials to cover areas of the assessments that are not emphasized in the curriculum. You can also design assessment measures that are better aligned with the learning emphasized in the curriculum to supplement your district's standard assessment package.

Approaches to Learning

Ultimately, you want to know about the kind of mathematical thinkers and learners that different curricula will help students become. To this end, you should examine curricula in terms of the learning opportunities they offer for students.

Equity: High Expectations for All Students

One goal of the NCTM *Standards* is that all students, not just top students, will be able to make sense of mathematics. Include selection criteria that focus on whether curriculum materials are engaging and comprehensible to a wide range of students, with lessons that offer multiple levels of challenge and multiple points of entry. Some of these entry points offer different ways to think about the mathematics to students with varying learning styles and intellectual strengths. Other entry points connect with students' different interests and backgrounds.

It is important for school texts in all subject areas to address equity by representing the diversity of our nation's students, and virtually all curricula have come a long way from the homogeneous perspective with which most of today's adults grew up. But there are much deeper issues at stake here than the question of whether a given student in your school will identify with a name or photograph on one of the pages of the textbook. The heart of the equity challenge posed by the *Standards* is to provide opportunities for all students to develop mathematically powerful ways of thinking without compromising the quality of the mathematics they study.

Active Student Involvement

Another fundamental premise of the *Standards* is that students should be actively involved in the construction of their own understanding. As you review curricula, look for the ways that they involve students in doing mathematics—developing mathematical ideas, testing them out, defending and proving them, and sharing their thinking with others. You should also look at how the supporting material helps teachers make sure that this involvement focuses on substantive mathematical ideas and not simply on working with a lot of "stuff." (Some people have distinguished between "hands-on" activities, which engage students with materials but may not elicit important mathematical ideas, and "minds-on" ones, which do engage students in significant mathematical thought.)

Try to imagine whether the lessons will capture the students' interest. Look at the contexts the curricula use for problems and investigations and determine whether they pose situations your students will care about. Will these contexts help your students make meaningful connections with mathematical ideas?

Presentation and Organization of Curriculum Materials

When you pick up a new mathematics book, the content is probably not the first thing you notice, even though it is the core of the curriculum. You are more apt to notice the way the materials look and feel—the color scheme, graphics, and layout. And while these are certainly not the most important factors in selecting a curriculum, they do matter in the day-to-day use of the materials.

There is more variability among standards-based programs in the organization and presentation of the materials than there is with more traditional textbooks. The curricula vary in their visual presentations. Some are done in four-color printing and others are not; some use photographs to illustrate the text and others use sketches and drawings.

They're also packaged in different ways. Some programs are published as year-long or semester-long student textbooks, some are available as a series of paperback modular units, and some come in both forms. While all are intended to be used as full-year curricula, the modular form allows them to be "unpackaged" and used one at a time or as supplements to textbooks that are already in use in your district. Some curricula that were originally developed as modular units are now packaged in book form, but retain some flexibility in the order in which units can be used during the year. (But you should pay close attention to developers' suggested ordering, as some educators have warned about taking a "mix and match" approach to using the individual modules on grounds that it risks undermining the mathematical coherence of the original sequencing. If you have questions, check with the developers about the kind of latitude in sequencing they advise.)

Users' preferences for these different forms of packaging vary. Modularized curricula may be more convenient for students to carry around, as they are less bulky and lighter than a full-sized textbook, but they may be easier to misplace. Of course, replacement costs for lost or damaged modules will probably be less than for full-year textbooks, as only individual units need to be repurchased. While the paperback modules are less durable, a student would use each module for only a couple of months during the year, so it's not clear which kind of packaging would ultimately prove longer-lasting.

Teacher guides show the same range of packaging options and again, preferences vary. Some teachers prefer having the units bound individually, finding individual units more convenient to locate and carry, and making it easier to focus on the specific work of the unit without distraction. Others would rather have access to the whole year's work so they can situate the unit in the full scope of the curriculum, referring back to ideas that precede the unit and ahead to those that follow. The curricula also differ in the type and amount of supporting material they provide for teachers. You may or may not find tips about organizing and implementing lessons, descriptions of the major mathematical goals for each unit, samples of student work, or problem solutions within the teacher's guide. Find out whether there are certain kinds of support your teachers really value and review curricula with these in mind.

Design and Use of Selection Criteria

Collecting Numbers or Impressions?

As you put together your criteria you will have to decide on the methods you will use to collect information about each curriculum. You have two major choices, which roughly correspond to the difference between multiple-choice and short-answer essay tests. The multiple-choice approach is more *quantitative*, relying heavily on numerical scores. The essay, or *qualitative*, approach relies primarily on descriptions of and judgments about the material.

When you take a quantitative approach you phrase your criteria as questions such as "yes or no?" or "how much/how often?" You assign numerical values or low/medium/high ratings as answers to these questions, and you then can compare curricula by tallying and comparing their scores. With a qualitative approach you answer questions by writing a series of short answers, phrasing your criteria as questions that ask "how," "why," or "where." You answer these questions by synthesizing your impressions of the curricula and organizing your observations into categories, supporting your evaluations with examples from the materials. We recommend a combination of both approaches.

Quantitative Assessments. A quantitative approach is good for those selection questions that are relatively straightforward. In general, the quantitative approach works well for questions that can be tallied or counted. It also offers a quick way to assess the degree of consensus about an analysis ("Were everyone's scores for this curriculum either 4 or 5?"). A quantitative approach can help you see general patterns of strengths and weakness within a curriculum and broadly characterize differences between curricula. You can easily summarize your ratings by graphing or charting scores and looking (literally) for patterns.

Many people prefer a number-based approach because it feels more objective to them—you can say that Curriculum A achieved a final score of 77 and Curriculum B scored 85, so Curriculum B "won." While such scoring schemes give the impression of objectivity (since they use numbers), most often it is, in fact, little more than that—an impression. There are several reasons why this is the case. First, it is rarely a cut-and-dried matter to assign a number to the questions you will be asking as you review different curricula. (How many times have you filled out 3-point scales on a questionnaire and puzzled over whether to answer "always" or "sometimes," while really wishing for a "sometimes/always" category?)

Because quantitative ratings don't directly reflect the thinking that goes into assigning a score or making a forced choice, it is difficult to know what a particular rating means: do two people who both assign a low score have the same reasons for doing so, or are they using different kinds of evidence for their judgments? When you rely heavily on number scores, either the reasoning that reviewers used to get to the numbers gets lost, or people have to recreate their decisions during committee discussions in order to elaborate on their scoring. So, paradoxically, taking time to jot down your analysis of different aspects of a curriculum may actually save you time. When the time comes to talk about curricula as a committee, you won't have to reconstruct your thinking from a rating sheet that's full only of numbers.

Qualitative Assessments. A qualitative approach is good for selection questions that are more complex and need more in-depth responses. Qualitative descriptions will help you create a more textured and nuanced view of the curricula you are reviewing and will encourage you to think hard about important issues of teaching and learning mathematics. Since part of making qualitative assessments involves explaining your reasoning and finding examples to support your judgments, using this approach prepares committee members to organize and articulate their views. These descriptions are also more informative on their own than simple rating scales are; it is possible for someone to read through a stack of qualitative reviews and get some sense of the particular approaches and characteristics of the different curricula.

The strength of the qualitative approach—its potential for textured descriptions and reasoned judgments—can also be its downside. The task of writing short narratives to many questions may feel overwhelming. This is a more time-consuming process, and, in the interest of being realistic and efficient, it is generally a good idea to suggest a limit to the time reviewers spend answering a set of qualitative selection questions.

Because the questions tend to be open ended, reviewers' responses can be fairly wide-ranging and can vary in their usefulness. This variability is often a result of the way the questions are posed. Vague or global questions generally yield less informative responses because they don't give the reviewers enough of a clue about what you actually want to know. Make sure that the questions are short and to the point. This will help reviewers focus and sharpen their responses. A series of specific questions about student learning, such as, "How does the curriculum help students learn to solve problems by working forward and backward ('doing' and 'undoing'); make conjectures and proofs; and formulate convincing arguments?" will be more likely to give you a sense of students' learning opportunities than the more global (and hence less well-defined) question, "How does the curriculum encourage students' active learning?"

Another potential problem with using a qualitative approach is that you can get buried in information without a clear idea of how to condense it into a manageable form. Read through committee members' evaluations and organize them by category, then make charts summarizing the comments that are relevant to each category. For example, make a category for "Student Interest" and, on a separate sheet for each curriculum, record all of the comments about how the curriculum engages students' interest. Make another category for "Student Thinking" and record all the comments about how different curricula encourage students to pursue mathematical ideas. Use these charts to organize committee members' judgments and to look for areas of strength and weakness within a curriculum, as well as make comparisons between different programs. These summary charts will also help identify issues that need further discussion in your committee.

Crafting Selection Questions

How do you put together a set of guiding questions that reflect the selection criteria you have established? In general, we suggest that you collect questions others have used and then customize them for your own situation—keep the ones that you think will help you to get at the important issues for your district, toss the questions that are irrelevant, and rework the ones that address good ideas but are not well-worded. For example, the question, "How will students coming from middle school be prepared to work with this high school curriculum?" is on the right track, but it's still a bit too general. Asking, "Will students coming from middle school have learned the requisite concepts and skills to work with this curriculum, and, if not, what won't they have learned?" is more specific and closer to the mark.

To start you on this process we propose some sample questions at the end of this chapter. Appendix 4 includes sample instruments from districts recently involved in curriculum selection, and the criteria developed by the U.S. Department of Education and by Project 2061 of the American Association for the Advancement of Science (AAAS).[6] These examples can give you an idea of the kinds of instruments that have been useful to people doing curriculum reviews.

Getting Up to Speed

We encourage you to practice applying your selection criteria to make sure that the members of your review committee are using them in the same way. One important part of this process is to discuss the assumptions about mathematics and mathematics learning and teaching that are implicit in your criteria. If you review curricula for "Student Communication," for example, do you mean that students have a chance to write in journals once a week, or that they should

---

[6] Project 2061 has used their criteria to analyze commonly used middle grades mathematics curricula. Reports of their results will be available through Project 2061, and also on their website, <http://project2061.aaas.org>.

offer solution strategies during whole-class discussion, or that they debate ideas with their classmates in small groups? We have found that it is common for people to adopt and use the language of reform, assuming that there is consensus about the meaning of the words, when, in fact, there are a wide variety of interpretations.

You can begin to make your assumptions explicit while the committee is putting together the criteria, and you can continue the conversation as you practice using the criteria on some of the curricula you will review. As you begin to see the criteria in action, you will see where you need to clarify or rework them.

You may want to practice using the criteria together before you begin your individual reviews, so that you can discuss your individual judgments and reasoning. (As noted earlier, this is like learning to play a card game by playing a few open hands with a running commentary.) Make sure that you discuss the places where you disagree or where there are uncertainties about how to respond to a question. This will help you develop consistency in reviewers' application of the criteria. The point is to get people feeling comfortable using the criteria as they look through materials and to make sure that everyone is using the criteria as reliably and consistently as possible, so that comparisons between reviewers will be meaningful.

Also, keep your selection criteria in mind when talking with teachers in your district who have worked with particular curricula, or with colleagues from other districts who have been looking into standards-based materials. You will find that you'll be able to focus your conversations better when you have identified specific issues about which you'd like to know more. Similarly, use your selection criteria to review teachers' impressions from any pilot testing you conduct.

Using Your Criteria to Make a Decision

In the end, your decision will rest on discussion among members of the selection committee and a considered judgment based on the range of information you have collected about the different curricula. There is no mathematical formula that will yield a foolproof decision about the right curriculum to choose; there are too many judgments to make that are incommensurate. If, for example, you judge a curriculum to be strong on mathematical processes but weak on teacher support, how do you come up with a summary statistic that reflects an objective weighting of these particular issues? Or if some members of your committee give a program high ratings on criteria that they don't personally value (though the district mathematics coordinator does) and then give the curriculum a low overall score, do you let this score stand or look for a way to factor in the ratings that were ignored? Your judgments about your priorities, goals, and resources will help you sort out the

> We ended up choosing [our curriculum] because it promoted deeper understanding of mathematics for students, a more systematic look at and take on the nature of mathematics, greater motivation for students, and access for students ranging from special needs students to the most advanced. This accessibility for all students was really important. In addition, the program was engaging and interesting for teachers to teach, and we had a deep conviction that it would improve student achievement. But improving scores wasn't the only criterion. If we were only concerned with the standardized test scores, we would have gone with another program. (J.G., assistant superintendent for curriculum and instruction)

responses to these kinds of questions—not calculating an average (or even weighted average) of the scores.

Frame your discussions of the curricula in terms of the following "big questions," using your curriculum reviews, discussions with teachers and other districts, and pilot data to support your judgments:

- What makes the mathematical content of the program strong?

- How does this curriculum match our vision for students' learning?

- Will our teachers be able to teach the program well?

- Can we afford to buy it and support its implementation? (This question is the focus of the next chapter, "Cost Considerations.")

Summary

Developing selection criteria and applying them to the curricula you are considering is a very important part of the selection process. The criteria are one way to focus and standardize your review of the programs under consideration and to organize information you may collect through other means (e.g., informal conversations with colleagues, classroom observations, and pilot testing).

When you design your selection criteria, make sure that you consider these important categories:

- mathematical content

- approaches to teaching

- approaches to learning

- presentation and organization of the curriculum materials

Careful crafting of selection criteria will help you make well-researched and well-planned curriculum choices.

Sample Selection Questions

We have included some sample questions below to help you get started on developing your own selection questionnaire. These questions all take a qualitative approach, and reviewers' answers should be supported with concrete examples from the curricula. This collection is not intended to be comprehensive or definitive, but rather to help you start developing your own questionnaire that will reflect your district's particular goals and emphases. See also Appendix 4 for samples of selection questions that other districts have used.

Mathematics Content

- What mathematics content is particularly well-developed in this program?

- Are there important mathematical ideas that students will not have a chance to develop adequately with this program? If so, what are they?

- How does the curriculum encourage the development of technical skills?

- How will this curriculum connect with the mathematics of curricula used in other grades?

    - Will students coming from (elementary school/middle school) have learned the requisite ideas and skills to work effectively with this curriculum? If not, what are the areas of weakness?

    - How does the mathematics that students will learn in this curriculum prepare them to progress to our (middle school/high school) curriculum or to college?

- How does the program fit with our curricula in other subject areas?

Pedagogy

- What instructional approaches does the curriculum use to encourage students' mathematical learning?

- How does the curriculum make mathematical concepts and skills accessible to students with different learning styles, backgrounds, and intellectual strengths?

- How does the curriculum help students learn to:

    - ask mathematically important questions?

    - make conjectures?

    - advance convincing arguments?

    - develop proofs?

Technology

- How does the curriculum's use of calculators and computers advance students' mathematical understanding?

- How will calculators and/or computers in this curriculum affect students development of technical and computational skills?

Assessment

- How does the program help teachers assess student learning for the purposes of instruction (e.g., homework, suggestions for discussion questions, quizzes)?

- What kinds of assessment opportunities does the curriculum offer for purposes of accountability (e.g., in-class performance, portfolios, individual and group projects)?

- What opportunities exist for students' self-assessment?

Teacher Support

- How does the program help teachers understand the important mathematical ideas of the curriculum?

- How does the program help teachers:

  - assist children with a range of abilities and learning styles develop mathematical understanding?

  - focus on advancing students' mathematical thinking?

  - encourage mathematical communication?

  - use technology effectively?

- What guidance does the curriculum offer teachers for communicating with parents and administrators?

- What kind of professional development—in content and pedagogy—will our staff need to teach this curriculum effectively?

- Will we have the necessary professional development resources to help teachers make these changes?

- Will our teachers find this an interesting curriculum to teach?

Organization and Structure of Materials

- What kinds of student and teacher materials come with the program?

- How are the materials organized? What are the advantages of the way(s) the materials are packaged?

- What additional materials (e.g., computers, classroom supplies) does the curriculum require?

- How does the organization of the curriculum create a coherent and comprehensible program?

- How do the supporting materials convey the organization and coherence of the curriculum to the teacher?

- How easy is it to use the materials?

    ~ Are the mathematical goals of the units and lessons clear?

    ~ What must teachers do to prepare for lessons?

    ~ Are the directions clear?

    ~ Are the materials needed for lessons readily available?

    ~ Are solutions to problem sets included?

CHAPTER 7

Cost Considerations

Curricula are "big ticket" items for a district, and projecting a budget for selection and implementation of a standards-based curriculum may involve taking into account costs that are not typically associated with traditional textbook adoptions. In addition to the cost of new textbooks, you can plan on additional expenses that derive in one way or another from pedagogical changes advocated by a standards-based approach. For example, the instructional techniques these new curricula employ—hands-on experiences, use of technology, and class discussions about students' work—assume that teachers have access to equipment and materials that may not currently be available in your schools.

It is also important to allocate resources for professional development to help teachers acquire these instructional techniques and the mathematical perspectives needed to promote students' learning. Because standards-based curricula challenge teachers to develop new classroom practices, the professional development needs associated with these kinds of programs are significantly greater than those of more traditional approaches. Professional development is a critical part of a successful adoption, and it is essential that you allocate adequate resources for it. This may mean increasing your professional development budget, or it may mean reviewing and reprioritizing your current professional development agenda to focus on mathematics. If you conclude that you will need to find additional funds to support the mathematics adoption, we encourage you to think of the expenses as investments in teachers and in mathematics reform. Future programs are likely to rely on a similar pedagogical model, so you can think of the expenses as start-up costs for the transition to reform-based teaching practice.

Both capital and operating budgets, and possibly grant and proposal writing, will be affected by the purchase of a new curriculum in ways that may be somewhat different than in past adoptions. Your selection and implementation of a standards-based program will, in turn, be influenced by your district's budgetary commitments and constraints. Some of the expenses associated with the purchase of a standards-based curriculum are straightforward, and others are less obvious. This chapter discusses district budgets in terms of the following considerations:

- capital and operating expenses

- supplementary funding sources (e.g., grants, entitlements, and awards)

- timing issues

Capital and Operating Expenses

The major capital expense in the purchase of a traditional curriculum is the cost of the textbooks. With standards-based programs there are additional costs to consider, as described below.

Curriculum Review

The review and selection process for standards-based programs is more time-consuming than in the past and may also involve initial training sessions to orient committee members to the philosophy and goals of mathematics education reform. Therefore, you may want to consider including some money in your budget for such costs as compensating selection committee members for their time or hiring consultants to advise the selection committee.

Professional Development for Teachers

It is difficult to overestimate the importance of professional development to the successful implementation of standards-based curricula. Because relatively few teachers are able to implement these new curricula fully without further professional development, it is essential that the adoption decision include a financial commitment to provide such support. (See Chapter 9, "Teacher Support," for a more in-depth discussion of professional development needs and resources.)

Professional development needs can be met in various ways, each of which will impact your budget differently. Districts have addressed professional development challenges in the following ways:

- publisher and/or curriculum developer training

- in-service workshops

- mathematics courses

- extended programs that focus on changing mathematics instruction

- release time for teacher leaders to mentor colleagues

- "special assignment" staff development positions for teacher leaders

- scheduling common preparation periods

- sharing of teaching responsibilities for new programs

These may seem like a lot of additional supports and corresponding costs to consider adding to your current professional development program, and you will want to select carefully among the options listed above. We can suggest two ways to think about providing teacher support. First, it *is* essential to recognize that adopting a standards-based curriculum will require your district to make a significant investment in professional development, but it is important to think about it as such—an investment in the professional skills of your teaching force and in the quality of your students' learning experiences.

Second, we encourage you to "think smart" about the ways you spend your professional development dollars. Research indicates that districts tend to be unsystematic in their allocation of professional development funds; one study found that the lack of a coherent professional development strategy resulted in significant expenditures (as much as 2–3 percent of a district's operating budget), with only fragmented and uncoordinated effects.[7] With no overall district strategy for leveraging individual teachers' staff development experiences for broader benefit, the effects of professional development expenditures were isolated, yielding little return on investment. By adopting a coherent strategy, consolidating and focusing resources on a well-articulated professional development goal, your district will be in a better position to make a real impact on teaching and learning.

Community Education

Many districts find that they incur expenses helping parents and other community members become acquainted and comfortable with standards-based mathematics programs. Among these are costs related to the following kinds of activities:

- parent information nights

- parent meetings with teachers and administrators

- creating and distributing sample lessons, handouts, weekly schedules, and explanations of the program

Manipulatives and Other Materials

Standards-based curricula call for the use of manipulatives (e.g., base 10 blocks, Unifix cubes, counting chips, geoboards, algebra tiles) and other materials (e.g., transparencies and pens for the overhead projector, paper clips, scissors, tape, graph paper), which have not traditionally been part of mathematics classrooms. Some of these materials may be required, and others suggested. Talk with publishers, curriculum developers, and teachers who are familiar with different curricula to find out which materials are essential to the various programs and which you may be able to do without. Also find out whether the manipulatives are included in the price of the curriculum or need to be purchased separately. Since many schools already have some kinds of manipulatives, you may need to inventory individual buildings to find out what you currently have and what your district would need to buy to support different curricula.

---

[7] For a discussion of the issues surrounding allocation of districts' professional development funds, see Miller, B., Lord, B., & Dorney, J. (1994). *Staff Development for Teachers: A Study of Configurations and Costs in Four Districts*. Newton, MA: Center for Learning, Teaching, and Technology, Education Development Center, Inc.

Calculators and Computers

Calculators are increasingly becoming a standard tool of mathematics programs at all levels. Four-function calculators are common in elementary schools and many middle school students are expected to use scientific calculators (and sometimes graphing calculators by the eighth grade). Graphing calculators are becoming integral to high school coursework in statistics and algebra. Some curricula also include computer-based lessons, which may require the purchase of software (e.g., geometry programs, spreadsheets, or supplementary, curriculum-specific software). As in the case of manipulatives, you will want to familiarize yourself with the technology demands of the particular curricula you are considering so that you can make accurate projections of equipment needs. Some districts ask students to buy their own calculators, providing assistance for those families unable to assume the cost themselves. Other districts buy sets of calculators for students to use in school. If your district will supply calculators for classroom use, or if the curricula you are considering include computer-based work, you will need to assess your current technology inventory and plans for technology-specific professional development, anticipate the technology demands your new curriculum will make, and factor these costs into your budget.

Overhead Projectors

Because overhead projectors are particularly useful in helping students illustrate their reasoning, present mathematical arguments, and share problem solutions that involve manipulatives, many programs recommend using overheads regularly during class discussions to supplement work at the blackboard. Few schools are currently equipped with overhead projectors for every classroom, or with carts that allow teachers to share them.

Classroom Furniture

Reform-based curricula assume that classrooms are configured in ways that support collaborative as well as individual work. Some districts have found it helpful to replace individual "tablet" desks or other classroom furniture with tables and chairs or movable desks so that teachers have the flexibility to move classroom furniture into different configurations, as needed.

Storage

The large number of components of standards-based programs, from manipulatives to multiple texts and workbooks, require storage space and shelving that may exceed your current capacity. This is particularly true for elementary and middle school curricula. You will also need to factor in adequate staff time and labor to keep track of the additional materials.

Replacement Costs

Replacement costs include both "consumables" (e.g., lined paper, graph paper, and journals) and curriculum materials (e.g., books and manipulatives) that are lost or destroyed. There are also personnel costs involved in inventorying, tracking, and reordering materials.

Photocopying Costs

The new curricula may require more photocopying than other mathematics programs you have used. Since photocopying has not historically been a significant expense, it may be easy to overlook. However, the increase in copying costs incurred by communicating with parents and reproducing blackline masters can be significant. Get estimates of photocopying costs from publishers and other districts using standards-based curricula and include these in your budget projections.

Supplementary Funding Sources

Assistance in funding the purchase of a standards-based program may be available through federal, state, and local sources.

Federal Funding

Both entitlement and competitive funds are available to help offset the costs incurred in adopting and implementing a new mathematics program.

Entitlement Funds

The following funds are available under the Improving America's Schools Act:

- *Title I* funds for the education of disadvantaged children

- *Title II (Eisenhower)* funds for professional development; a portion of these moneys is dedicated specifically to professional development in mathematics, science, and technology. (See Appendix 3 for contact information for U.S. Department of Education-funded Regional Laboratories and Eisenhower Regional Consortia.)

- *Title VI* funds to support innovative programs

If your district serves a community in which more than 50 percent of the student population lives below the poverty level, you are allowed to pool entitlement funds to support schoolwide programs. Pooling of funds offers greater flexibility in allocating moneys to the various costs associated with adopting standards-based mathematics programs.

Competitively Awarded Funds

- There are several competitive programs available through the National Science Foundation for districts that have developed a coherent, systemwide plan to improve mathematics, science, and technology education. *Urban Systemic Initiative (USI)*, *Local Systemic Change (LSC)*, and *Rural Systemic Initiative (RSI)* grants are awarded to urban, midsized, and rural districts, respectively. If you are interested in applying for one of these grants, you can contact the National Science Foundation for information.

- *Comprehensive School Reform Demonstration Program (CSRD)* is a new funding stream targeted for implementation of research-based school reform models. It is administered through state departments of education. You can contact your regional Comprehensive Assistance Center for guidance about pursuing this federal funding source (see Appendix 3 for a list of contacts at these centers).

Publisher Incentives

Publishers frequently offer incentives, such as supplementary materials or a certain number of training days, as part of a curriculum purchase. In general, once a district has made a purchase the publishers will send representatives to help teachers become acquainted with the organization of the curriculum and to provide some basic guidance for implementation. Some companies provide even more in the way of professional development, such as day-long workshops or week-long summer institutes. These incentives can help offset some small portion of the costs of materials or initial professional development expenses.

Raising Community Dollars

Local organizations and businesses are often willing to contribute small amounts of money to districts' efforts to improve mathematics education. These small grants can be especially useful for purchasing materials or offsetting photocopying costs. When the community makes a financial contribution to offset some of the costs of the new curriculum, you also receive a secondary benefit in the form of community commitment to the curriculum's success. Consider soliciting contributions from these groups:

- community education foundations

- local businesses

- parent-teacher organizations

Timing Issues

Budgetary issues can affect the program selection and implementation process in some subtle ways. For example, we have emphasized that planning for selection and implementation of standards-based programs requires more time than districts have typically allotted in the past. Yet many districts must purchase curriculum materials within a single fiscal year in order to ensure that they will have the funds needed for the adoption. Thus, the time frame dictated by the budget may be inconsistent with the time frame necessary for the most careful analysis of potential curricula or for preparing teachers to learn to implement the new curriculum effectively.

This inconsistency can lead to a difficult dilemma: should you invest in a curriculum that is somewhat beyond teachers' current experience and comfort levels because you believe that, once teachers have learned to implement it, the program will offer your students the best mathematics education? If you make this choice, will the curriculum be overwhelming to teachers and sit unused in their classrooms? Alternatively, should you decide on a somewhat less challenging curriculum that you expect will be used for a relatively short time as the district prepares to move on to even more challenging standards-based curricula? Different districts have different answers to these questions.

One possible solution is to phase in the curriculum over time, both fiscally and in terms of implementation. If you do consider this strategy, it is critical that you secure and maintain a strong central office commitment to the program phase-in. Without this commitment, changing priorities or the press of new or unexpected budget crises can lead to a redirection of funds originally allocated for the rolling implementation of the new mathematics curriculum.

Summary

The question "Can we afford the program we want?" involves looking beyond the initial purchase price of new texts and teacher guides to a number of additional expenses. Primary among these is the cost of professional development for your teachers. Professional development is absolutely essential to the success of your implementation effort, and it is at least as important as your investment in the curriculum materials themselves. There are other costs as well, such as outfitting classrooms with the supplementary materials students will need to make full use of the curriculum.

These additional costs can seem formidable; indeed, they reflect expenses that you do not necessarily associate with a textbook adoption cycle. Consolidate and leverage those funds currently available to you to support the adoption and seek additional funding if necessary. The expense is an investment in the future of mathematics education—part of the cost of moving toward standards-based mathematics instruction.

CHAPTER 8

Piloting

At some point in your selection process, often after you have narrowed down your choices to a few candidates, you will want to get better acquainted with certain curricula. You have a good idea which materials look best on paper, but you also need to know how they fare when transformed into classroom instruction. As one mathematics curriculum specialist put it, "Will these materials work with our students, and how will teachers react to them?"

Many districts include a piloting phase in their selection process, in which some teachers use the candidate curricula on a trial basis and provide feedback about their classroom experiences. Selection committees (or district decision makers) then use these results to make an official selection. In other districts the term piloting has become synonymous with the early stages of implementation, referring to post-selection efforts that help teachers learn how to teach the curriculum effectively.

In this guide we refer to piloting as a phase associated with the latter part of the selection process (although much of the information that pilots provide has to do with the implementation challenges posed by different curricula). Be aware, though, that in other contexts people may talk about piloting as an earlier component of the selection process or as a preliminary step in implementation.

At whatever point in the process a district uses piloting, the strategy of monitoring early efforts to work with new curricula serves a variety of purposes:

- seeing the materials in action

- building teachers' interest and buy-in

- increasing district familiarity with the programs

- identifying professional development needs

- creating a cadre of experienced lead teachers

> *Once the pilot got started with the kindergarten, first, and second grade teachers, other teachers in the school were fascinated. (C.U., associate superintendent for curriculum and instruction)*

There are several advantages to including a piloting phase in your selection process. One is that it provides information about how teachers and students in your district will actually work with the curricula you are considering. You can find out whether the curricula play out in the classroom the way you imagined they would; for example, does the curriculum that looked like it would really intrigue students actually capture their interest? Piloting can give you information about how comfortable your teachers will be with the new program and how effective it will be in helping students develop into powerful mathematical

> *Give teachers time to really try something. They use a couple of units and then see how they're part of a whole comprehensive program. And teachers are at really different places, so the extra time is so valuable. (E.B., mathematics curriculum supervisor)*

thinkers. Piloting can reveal unforeseen problems or pleasant surprises. If you pilot more than one curriculum you can compare how well they promote student achievement of district goals and standards.

The pilot phase also serves as a trial run, helping prepare the district for a full-scale implementation. It offers the opportunity for teachers to begin to develop both familiarity with the materials and a sense of ownership. When curriculum decisions are driven by teacher interest rather than administrative recommendation alone, the commitment to successful implementation is greater.

Another advantage of piloting is that it can be used to build teacher leadership—teachers who have used the curriculum in the classroom and/or have worked on implementation issues with others in and outside the district can share their experiences with their colleagues. These experiences provide information about the kinds of policies and support that will help make implementation a success. Pilot teachers who have become familiar with the curriculum will also be able to serve as resources for their colleagues during implementation. Many districts find that this extra time to learn about working with the curriculum is valuable preparation for full-scale implementation.

Piloting Strategies

In this section we describe three basic strategies for piloting materials. Each has its advantages and disadvantages; one approach may be better than the other for meeting your district's particular needs. Whichever strategy you choose, make sure that the teachers who pilot materials are familiar with both the philosophy and the pedagogical approach behind standards-based curricula. If not, they will need some professional development prior to using the curricula. Many of the publishers offer orientations, institutes, workshops, or other training specifically for their materials. In addition, you will want to plan for professional development and support for these teachers during the piloting phase itself. This may involve scheduling common preparation time for teachers in the same building or arranging regular meetings with a staff developer, during which teachers discuss the teaching and learning promoted by the curriculum.

Different Pilot Groups for Each Finalist Curriculum

One strategy is to select a different group of teachers to pilot each of the finalist curricula for an extended period of time—one year, if possible. These pilot teachers can meet throughout the year and then report to the committee about their experiences. The advantage of this approach is that teachers get in-depth experience with the curriculum they are piloting. They have a chance to see how mathematical ideas develop over the course of a whole year, and they have time to become familiar with the curriculum's pedagogical approach. A disadvantage of separate pilot groups is that teachers may find it difficult to compare the curricula when they are only familiar with one of them. In one large district, for example, teachers were so strongly attached to the curriculum they had piloted themselves that it was not possible to reach consensus on a selection. They had to plan a second phase of piloting, during which selected teachers taught a unit from the other candidate curriculum in order to make comparisons.

It is possible to use this piloting strategy for a shorter period of time—for example, piloting several units instead of the whole year's curriculum. However, shortening the amount of time that teachers work with a curriculum compromises the major strength of this strategy—the opportunity for in-depth experience with the materials.

Teachers Pilot All Contenders

Another strategy is to ask interested teachers to pilot all of the finalists, which eliminates the problem of teachers becoming attached to "their" particular curriculum. In one very elaborate variation on this strategy a district that was piloting three curricula had each pilot teacher work with two of the three programs. Teachers taught a unit from one program in the fall and a unit from a second program in the spring. This strategy gave teachers the chance to work with more than one curriculum but avoided their settling on a single favorite. When it came time to discuss reactions to the curricula, teachers had to listen carefully to each others' assessments because there was always one group of teachers with no personal experience with the curriculum under discussion. Teachers, however, were able to judge their colleagues' comments about the unfamiliar curriculum in terms of their comments about the materials they had both reviewed. The disadvantage of this approach is that teachers have less time to see how ideas are developed or how students respond to the materials throughout the curriculum. Depending on how similar the curricula are to each other, changing programs several times over the course of the year may also run the risk of creating some discontinuity in instruction for students.

I learned the hard way that each pilot teacher has to pilot both selections—otherwise they will nearly always vote for the one they've tried. It's like test-driving only one new car, when you're used to driving an old clunker around town. Of course the new car is the best thing to come down the pike! We ran two staff developments for subgroups of pilot teachers who each taught both pilot programs. It was a nine-week rotation—half the teachers trained to pilot one program while the other half trained to pilot the other; then after nine weeks they switched and repeated the training process to pilot the other program for another nine weeks. (V.M., mathematics, science, and technology supervisor)

Piloting a Provisional Selection

Some districts undertake a pilot phase as a final test of the curriculum they have provisionally selected and hope to implement districtwide. Since districts using this strategy are already prepared to commit to adopting the curriculum they are piloting, this phase may be focused more heavily on *how* to make the curriculum work rather than *whether* it will work in the district. The strength of this approach lies in the high degree of district interest in the materials. However, districts using this strategy must be prepared for the possibility that the pilot will lead to a rejection of the curriculum and need to allow enough time for another round of selection.

The teachers decided to pilot [a curriculum that looked like a compromise between one that was too 'paper and pencil' and one that was too activities oriented], with the hope of implementing it. The teachers were dissatisfied on many accounts. They felt the program didn't hang together, spiraled out of control, and was just a collection of activities without cohesiveness. The Math Committee got together again and re-quested that [the district] expand the pilot to include proven programs with good field testing and consistency across grade levels. They gathered information about implementation models and reevaluated the alignment of each program with a few of the content strands in their district standards. (P.D., curriculum and assessment coordinator)

Selecting Pilot Teachers

Some districts have piloted materials with as few as two or three teachers; large districts may use more than 100 pilot teachers. How many you choose will depend, among other factors, on the size of your district, your need to cultivate teacher buy-in, and the number of teachers who are ready and willing to bring a new curriculum into the classroom. The potential drawback of a very small pilot effort is that your information may have more to do with the particular successes and difficulties of specific teachers than with the robustness and power of the materials themselves. Your choice of pilot teachers depends on your particular goals. For example, if you want information about how effective the curriculum can be, you should select pilot teachers who subscribe to the goals of mathematics education reform, are strong mathematically, and are versed in new pedagogical approaches. On the other hand, if you want to learn how the average teacher will use the materials and what kind of support teachers in the district will need to implement the different curricula, you should select teachers who represent the range of instructional approaches and mathematical sophistication in your district.

Some districts focus their piloting on a single school. One advantage of this approach is that the teachers can work as a team, meeting to discuss their experiences and working together to iron out kinks they may encounter. Other districts open up the piloting process to any interested teachers in the district. One large urban district wanted to ensure that the pilot information they collected was representative of the district as a whole, so they chose pilot teachers from every grade level, from schools where student achievement varied, and from schools that reflected the economic and ethnic diversity of the community.

Some districts make sure that teachers on the selection committee participate in the piloting, while in other districts the pilot teachers may report to the committee but do not serve as members. When teachers on the selection committee are among those piloting the curriculum, they can draw on the experiences and knowledge derived from their dual roles in arriving at a final choice.

Some districts try to have teachers from every grade level pilot materials, while others pilot in only one or two grades. The advantage of piloting in a number of grades is that you can learn how the program unfolds across the grade span.

Assessing Your Pilot Phase

If you are piloting curricula in order to choose among possible finalists, you will evaluate the results of the pilot phase according to the same selection criteria you used earlier in the process (see Chapter 6, "Developing and Applying Selection Criteria"). When you were first reviewing curricula for possible consideration, you had only your analyses of the written materials and possibly reports from others about their experiences to go on. Now that teachers in your district have used some of the materials themselves, you have classroom-based data to inform your decision.

Collect information from teachers about their experiences and have selection committee members observe classrooms using the pilot programs. Use your pilot phase to collect information about the original selection criteria categories:

- mathematics content

- approaches to teaching

- approaches to learning

- presentation and organization of the curriculum materials

In addition, use the pilot phase to gather information about responses to the curricula and potential implementation issues:

- teacher, student, and parent perceptions of the curricula

- student performance

- resources and support that will be needed for successful implementation

- overall strengths and weaknesses of the curricula

The Choice Not to Pilot

Although districts commonly use information about classroom piloting to inform their selection decisions, it is not a universal practice. There are a variety of reasons that a district might arrive at a selection without piloting. Decision makers might believe they have enough information to make a choice without taking the time to pilot. If there is district opposition to adopting a standards-based curriculum, the administration may feel that a pilot would only increase resistance and therefore move forward on a selection without pilot information. And some experienced mathematics administrators are skeptical about the validity of pilot information for decision-making purposes.

If your own circumstances lead you to select a curriculum without a piloting phase, remember that piloting also serves as a trial run of the materials for implementation, and as an important source of information for planning professional development. If you do not pilot during the selection process, you should plan on piloting as part of early implementation in order to accomplish the following:

- Identify and resolve some of the logistical and technical challenges of using the curriculum.

- Identify professional development needs for full-scale implementation and develop plans to provide the necessary support.

- Increase community interest in and support for the curriculum by giving people an opportunity to see it in action in some district classrooms.

Summary

Piloting functions as a "test drive" for a curriculum. It offers a naturalistic laboratory for evaluating how a curriculum translates into everyday classroom work and enables you to become better acquainted with its opportunities and challenges. The information you gather from piloting will help you plan your implementation and, if you use piloting as a selection strategy, make a final selection decision. Decisions about the structure and extent of piloting involve various tradeoffs. Your district's particular goals, needs, and resources will guide your decisions about when and how to pilot.

Part III
Curriculum Implementation

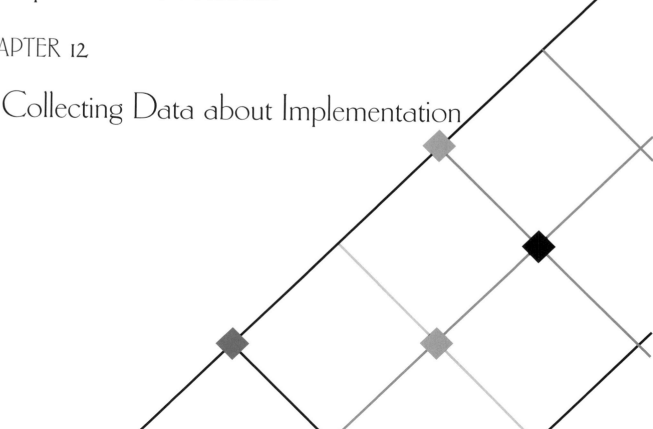

Part III

Curriculum Implementation

Your district may be accustomed to implementing new curricula districtwide in the fall of the school year following a selection decision. With standards-based curricula, selection is frequently just the first step of a longer, multi-year implementation effort. Once you have chosen a new curriculum, plan its implementation carefully and strategically to ensure that you achieve your district's goals. The importance of thinking long term about implementation is not unique to standards-based mathematics curricula—it is common sense and good practice. But because the content, pedagogy, and organization of these curricula are likely to have unfamiliar elements for teachers, a thoughtful selection process and a strategic plan for implementing the materials are *essential* for success.

> *Implementation is your key phase. [It is the time you provide the most intensive] support for teachers and also continue to drive and monitor the curriculum implementation. It takes time, money, and people. It's hard, but it's **so** important. (M.D., K–12 district mathematics supervisor)*

When you adopt a standards-based curriculum, you cannot expect teachers to walk into their classrooms at the beginning of the year ready to use the new materials. These curricula are different enough from traditional programs that teachers will need in-depth opportunities to learn about the new content and instructional practices, sufficient preparation time to assimilate these new aspects, and support while they are teaching it. The necessary preparation and professional development will take time and resources. When you anticipate the need for a more extended implementation period and plan for it in advance, you will be able to provide teachers with the support they need and also help administrators, parents, and other stakeholders in the community become accustomed to the curriculum.

Another important consideration in your implementation plan is choosing a strategy for bringing the curriculum implementation to full scale. Do you start with one grade level or one school the first year and then add on the next year? Do all teachers teach several units of a curriculum the first year and then teach the whole curriculum the following year? Preparing for full implementation is best done hand-in-hand with the design of professional development offerings and teacher support. This part of the guide deals with the central issues of curriculum implementation: providing teacher support, securing community support, achieving full-scale implementation, and collecting data about the implementation process.

CHAPTER 9

Teacher Support

Now that your district has selected a new curriculum, your teachers face the challenge of learning to make the materials work well in their classrooms. When you select a standards-based curriculum, chances are that it looks and feels quite different from the mathematics programs your teachers have used in the past. In addition, it contains new mathematical ideas and pedagogical approaches that teachers must master. They will need help learning to use these new curricula effectively and in a way that is consistent with the intentions of the developers.

In this chapter we discuss some general principles for designing effective staff support and some strategies that districts have used. Briefly, the principles are as follows:

[Most] teachers will need a tremendous amount of initial, as well as ongoing, assistance to implement any standards-based curriculum. This is a critical issue to address. There needs to be a strong, up-front assurance that professional development will be available. (M.B., professional development consultant)

- Think of teacher support as a long-term prospect—in terms of months and years, rather than days.

- Expect teachers' needs for support to change as implementation progresses.

- Budget for professional development and other forms of teacher support—they cost money.

- Be strategic—develop a coherent plan for professional development that does the following:

    - responds to your teachers' needs

    - leverages your costs

    - addresses issues of scaling up to full implementation within your district

Teacher Support is a Long-Term Prospect

Learning to implement standards-based curricula effectively takes time, and you should expect that teachers will need more support in the first few years of implementation than you are typically used to providing for new curriculum adoptions. Most teachers need to make significant changes in their classroom practice in order to fully implement a new standards-based curriculum. The curricula are demanding to teach, offering challenges to teachers on many levels. The structure and organization of units and lessons are different in standards-based curricula than in programs they have used before; the

Textbook companies will help you the year you adopt, but it's really a matter of working the implementation support into your long-range plan of how to improve mathematics teaching over time. (E.B., mathematics curriculum supervisor)

mathematical ideas are developed in different kinds of contexts and they thread throughout the year (or even throughout the entire multi-year curriculum) differently than they do in typical textbooks; some of the mathematical content itself may be new to teachers; and the pedagogical approaches, with their emphasis on doing mathematics—observing, conjecturing, testing, problem solving and discussing mathematical ideas—are often unfamiliar.

With all these challenges, teachers won't become confident and skilled users of standards-based curricula with only one or two half-day workshops. It will take time and support for teachers to meet the different layers of challenge that these curricula present, which is to be expected. Districts choose standards-based curricula *because* the materials involve different approaches to mathematics learning and teaching, so it stands to reason that teachers will need some time and assistance in learning how to use the new approaches effectively. Nothing will contribute more to the successful implementation of your curriculum than ongoing support of the teachers who are responsible for transforming the written materials into actual occasions for learning in the classroom.

Changing Support Needs

Teachers need different kinds of support at different points in the implementation process. As teachers become better acquainted with the new curriculum and its goals for students' mathematics learning, they will encounter different sets of challenges. You can think of implementation needs as falling into roughly three time periods:

- pre-implementation

- early implementation

- ongoing implementation

Pre-Implementation: Raising Awareness

Many districts find it useful to begin professional development before teachers are asked to use the new curriculum, particularly if general awareness about the ideas and rationale behind mathematics education reform among teachers is low. (If you have worked with the "Concerns-Based Adoption Model" [CBAM], which articulates different stages of concern during implementation of an innovation, you will recognize this as Stage 0: Basic Awareness of the Innovation.)[8] You can use the time prior to actual implementation to orient teachers to the goals and methods of standards-based programs. Offer teachers introductory

---

[8] Recent discussions of this model can be found in Driscoll, M., & Bryant, D. (1998). *Learning About Assessment, Learning Through Assessment.* Washington, DC: National Academies Press; Loucks-Horsley, S., Hewson, P.W. , Love, N., & Stiles, K.E. (1998). *Designing Professional Development for Teachers of Science and Mathematics.* Thousand Oaks, CA: Corwin Press; and Loucks-Horsley, S., & Stiegelbauer, S. "Using Knowledge of Change to Guide Staff Development" in Lieberman, A. & Miller, L., Eds. (1991). *Staff Development for Education in the 90's.* New York: Teachers College Press (pp. 15-36).

information and provide opportunities for mathematical exploration that will give them personal experiences in which to ground discussions about teaching and learning mathematics. Also encourage them to visit classrooms where teachers are using the new curriculum. During this time, many districts also offer professional development focusing on mathematical content knowledge and pedagogical practices. This kind of ongoing professional development can build a strong foundation for a successful implementation.

Early Implementation: "Just in Time" Professional Development

When it is time to unwrap the teacher's edition, find storage space for the new collections of manipulatives, and figure out how to introduce the first lesson of the year, teachers suddenly find that they are faced with a host of practical, detailed questions that couldn't easily be anticipated by a theoretical understanding of the curriculum. It can take a year (or even two or three) for teachers to feel as if they have mastered the mechanics of a standards-based program.

Because these curricula explore mathematical ideas through a variety of activities and materials, lessons have many moving parts—manipulatives, calculators and/ or computers, different kinds of working groups, journals, and worksheets. It is challenging to organize and coordinate all of these parts, and teachers who are new to standards-based curricula often have very real and pressing questions, for example, what materials will I need to pull together for this activity? what preparation do I need to do? what black-line masters will I need to get photocopied? how many computer stations do I need for this lesson, and what do students work on when it's not their turn at the computer? Some teachers also need time to become accustomed to the instructional model embedded within these curricula, for example, starting with a contextually based problem or managing the "Launch–Explore–Summarize" organization of mathematical investigations.[9]

Pacing is another issue that teachers universally encounter in the first year or two of implementation. Many teachers find that standards-based curricula are very rich and that there is much more material than a class can actually complete in a single year. It may be difficult for teachers to anticipate the amount of time it will take to complete units, since so much of the pacing of lessons depends on student-generated activity, rather than teacher-generated lecture and demonstration. Teachers are faced with the need to make decisions about where to focus class time and where they can skip material without sacrificing important student learning. Many teachers have found it very useful to work through lessons themselves before class in order to clarify the mathematical focus of the

---

[9] This organization is presented in the middle grades curriculum *Connected Mathematics*, published by Cuisenaire • Dale Seymour. In the "launch" phase the teacher establishes a context for the problem the class is to investigate. Students work to solve the problem during the "explore" phase, and the "summarize" phase serves as the occasion for students to discuss their work, deepen their understanding, and make connections to other mathematical ideas. Other curricula use variants of the same process.

unit and anticipate some of the issues and ideas their students may bring to the lessons. Actually working through the activity also helps teachers recognize new ideas in the mathematics they have been teaching, or articulate previously unexplored connections among mathematical ideas.

Even with this kind of preparation, pacing decisions are still difficult to make the first or second time through the curriculum, as teachers cannot yet draw on their prior experience with the ways lessons unfold in the classroom. They will need guidance to help them identify those lessons that are central for developing important mathematics and those that are more ancillary or supplementary, and to understand how mathematical ideas play out throughout the year. This is particularly a challenge for curricula that "spiral," revisiting ideas over the course of the year rather than providing all of the instruction geared toward a particular idea in a single unit. Without experience in how a curriculum develops spiraling ideas over time, teachers have difficulty knowing when they can let go of something for the time being because students will meet up with it again later in the year or at another grade level. Once teachers have worked their way through the curriculum a few times, pacing issues generally become more manageable.

At the same time that teachers are working to become acquainted with the curriculum, they often are called on to explain (and sometimes defend) it to their students' parents. Teachers who are already familiar with standards-based curricula and invested in the general approach may not find it particularly difficult to represent the new curriculum to parents, but teachers who are just learning about the curriculum themselves may have some trouble. You can support teachers in this task by offering concrete suggestions for productive ways to work with parents, and preparing others in the district (e.g., principals, mathematics supervisors, and mathematics department heads) to assume some of this responsibility.

Meeting "Just in Time" Implementation Needs

There is an immediacy to these kinds of implementation concerns. Feeling comfortable and in control of the mechanics of any particular lesson can make the difference between having the class flow smoothly and having it feel like a train wreck. Having a clear sense of pacing helps teachers make decisions about the amount of time to spend on individual lessons. Teachers who are wrestling with these kinds of logistics need practical, "just in time" support to help them manage the curriculum and direct more of their attention to the mathematical agenda. You can help provide this kind of support in a number of ways:

- Negotiate professional development with the curriculum's publisher as part of the district's purchase package. Many publishers do conduct introductory workshops to orient teachers to the program. (Curriculum developers may provide similar kinds of support, as well as more in-depth training, through the satellites of the NSF-funded curriculum implementation centers; see Appendices 1 and 2 for contact information.)

- Help teachers develop images of standards-based instruction by arranging for them to consult with experienced users in other schools and/or districts and, if possible, visit their classrooms. You may also be able to get videotapes of lessons from the curriculum publisher or the appropriate satellite implementation center.

- Make sure that teachers have access to consultations with teacher coaches, mentors, mathematics supervisors, or other trained district personnel when they have questions or problems with implementation.

- Hold regular grade-level meetings about teachers' implementation experiences. These meetings provide a venue for teachers to work together on implementation issues, provide support for each other, and learn as a team.

- Schedule common preparation times so teachers can meet regularly to share experiences, plan and debrief lessons, and generally support each other's efforts. Other than actually coteaching, no other formal form of support is as ongoing and as tied to the daily details of the curriculum as regularly preparing lessons together.

- Provide teachers with a scope and sequence guide that is keyed specifically to the new curriculum. This guide will help teachers identify lessons that address skills and concepts of particular importance to the district and make decisions about pacing.

- Develop guidelines and/or materials to help teachers talk with parents about the new curriculum.

There need to be support groups for teachers, where they can share their experiences and really talk about what it's like to use the materials— what's working and what's not. Structures need to be in place; some stuff can happen districtwide, but it's really important for things to be together at the school level. (K. A., regional LSC director)

The school has to make a commitment to give teachers some kind of release time so the teachers can deal with bringing this new stuff into their lives, because it is a big change. (M.N., high school teacher leader)

We've tried to develop a document that describes the big ideas in each of the units, indicating when students should have mastery of particular ideas. We've collected data from teachers' classrooms, using these materials to supplement what we got from the units, i.e., examples of student work. We'll be using it with parents and new teachers. (J.F., K–12 mathematics coordinator)

Ongoing Implementation: Deepening Mathematical Understanding and Developing Classroom Practice

Once teachers have become familiar with their new curriculum and are less preoccupied with the details of setting up and carrying out the individual lessons, they can turn their attention more fully to consideration of the pedagogical and mathematical innovations that are part of standards-based curricula. For many teachers, this means exploring new ways of thinking about mathematics as a body of knowledge, what it means to know or understand mathematics, and how best to promote mathematical learning. Teachers begin to move away from concerns about the mechanics of lessons, and become more attentive to questions about their students' learning.

Focusing on Student Learning

Below are examples of questions that characterize teachers' shifting attention from implementing the logistics and mechanics of a standards-based curriculum to facilitating students' mathematical thinking.

SAMPLE QUESTIONS ABOUT LOGISTICS	SAMPLE QUESTIONS ABOUT STUDENT LEARNING
• How can I allot enough class time for students to finish their group work and also have a class discussion? • What kind of homework can I assign when students are at such different places in their explorations? • When should my students be working in groups and when should they work on their own? • Where should I keep manipulatives so students can have access to them without disrupting their classmates' work?	• How do I know whether a discussion is moving in a mathematically productive direction? • What kinds of questions can I ask students that won't be leading but will nonetheless guide them to further their mathematical understanding? • What important mathematical ideas do I want students to take from this unit, and how does this specific lesson advance their understanding of those ideas? • What did Sylvia and Hector mean when they said that 1/2 could sometimes be bigger than 1/3 and sometimes smaller?

During this time, teachers need professional development that will help them deepen their understanding of the mathematics in the curriculum and develop more effective means of facilitating student learning. To some extent, the new curricula themselves will stimulate teachers to consider these issues. But, while the programs can help raise issues and challenges for teachers, they cannot by themselves help teachers resolve them. For this, more extensive professional development is needed.

*In the first year we were dealing with classroom implementation: "How do I get started with the curriculum, how do I organize, how do I deal with correcting all the homework?" In the second year teachers were ready for more content development. The materials are rich with mathematics content information. It's there if the teachers are able to read it and take it in [without being overwhelmed by the logistics of the program]. They need to have the chance to take a summer institute on content, **after** the first year. (M.T., K–8 mathematics supervisor)*

Mathematics

Some of the mathematical content of standards-based programs, as well as the contexts in which this content is presented, may be new and unfamiliar to teachers. With lessons framed as challenges, for example, to design efficient floor plans, develop ciphers and codes, or plan for a long journey, the mathematical concepts that drive lessons may not always be apparent. Teachers may need help drawing connections between the activities and the mathematics that motivates them. They may also need help learning to increase their emphasis on engaging students in mathematical processes—reasoning, problem solving, communicating, and making mathematical connections. Because much of the instruction with standards-based curricula occurs through interaction in the classroom instead of lectures and individual seatwork, teachers need to be more aware of whether the ideas that students are developing in their explorations and discussions are important and actually worth pursuing. Using these new curricula, teachers are called on to think more about how their students' ideas are building toward greater mathematical understanding.

> *I'm starting to think that adopting the most forward-thinking curriculum is foolhardy without the appropriate teacher support. Teacher readiness for materials is key. It needs to happen early on, and teachers need . . . support over time, on both the content and the pedagogy. I'm finding that there are a lot of teachers who don't know [all of] the mathematics behind the activities. (K.A., regional LSC director)*

In the past teachers have not generally been called on to develop these kinds of judgments about mathematics, and it will take time for them to learn to do so. Standards-based materials require teachers to have a firm grasp on the important mathematical ideas that underlie the curriculum and an understanding of how children develop these ideas. They also require teachers to understand the connections between these ideas and the individual activities and to recognize the possibilities for student learning in materials that do not look like traditional lessons. For some teachers, this means deepening their own understanding of the mathematics they teach.

Pedagogy

When you enter a mathematics classroom at any grade level that is using standards-based materials, the activity in the room may seem quite foreign compared to your own mathematics classroom experiences. If you were to visit a class involved in a small group activity, you would find students freely moving about the room, talking with each other, and maybe even arguing heatedly. The teacher would be moving among these groups, checking in with students about what they were finding and asking questions to direct their work toward the major mathematical ideas of the lesson. If your visit coincided with a class discussion, students might be responding to questions from the teacher, sharing a problem solution at the overhead projector or blackboard, explaining the reasoning behind their ideas, or asking each other questions. And if you were to visit when students were working individually, you might nonetheless see them going to classmates with questions or sharing observations and ideas.

Because so much of the mathematics work in standards-based classrooms happens in the context of interactions, teachers must learn to draw mathematical learning out of the flow of ideas going on around them. They must learn to recognize important mathematical ideas as they come up and know how to take advantage of "teachable moments." They struggle with when to offer students guidance and when to leave them to their own process of exploration and discovery. They need to learn how to uncover students' ideas, drawing them out toward a more developed understanding. These ways of working are learned through experience, thoughtful reflection, discussion with colleagues, and professional development.

Facilitating Classroom Learning

The following vignette depicts a typical scene in a standards-based classroom.

Mrs. Martinez and Mr. Golden, who have teamed up to teach eighth grade this year, have divided their students into groups of four. The teachers have challenged them to show why the text says that division by zero is "undefined." The teachers want their students to know "why you can't divide by zero." Once the students figure out why division by zero is undefined, they are to prepare something that they could use to justify their explanation to the rest of the class.

Mrs. Martinez suggests that the calculator may be a useful tool for this problem. "Making up some kind of story problem for the situation that involves division might be helpful for others," adds Mr. Golden. The two teachers have arranged their large classroom so that calculators, graph paper, Unifix cubes and base 10 blocks, felt-tip markers and blank overhead transparencies, rulers, and other materials are out where students can freely use them. This facilitates the use of alternative tools. Students are encouraged and expected to make decisions about which tool to use. Several students are . . . preparing overheads to display their conclusions about division by zero. Others are excitedly punching buttons [on their calculators].

"The answer keeps getting larger and larger!" exclaim a pair of girls as they watch the results obtained by successively dividing 4 by smaller and smaller divisors with the calculator. "Why is that important?" asks Mrs. Martinez as she watches over one girl's shoulder. "Well, because each of the numbers we are dividing by is getting closer and closer to zero but isn't zero." "Maybe you could make a graph to show what you are finding," suggests Mrs. Martinez.

Mr. Golden finds two students slouching sullenly in their chairs behind the room divider. "We don't understand what to do," grumbles one. Sitting down next to them, Mr. Golden begins, "Let's see if I can help. You are trying to figure out what the special problem is in trying to divide by zero. Maybe you can use some things you already know about division. How do you know that $8 \div 2$ is 4? How could you prove that if someone challenged your answer?" The students look at him disbelievingly. He waits. Then one says, "Well, I'd just say that 4 times 2 is 8 so 8 divided by 2 has to be 4." "Can that help you at all with this problem?" asks Mr. Golden. He stands up. The two students look at one another and then, sitting up a bit, begin talking. "Well, that doesn't work if you take $8 \div 0$," Mr. Golden hears as he walks away. [10]

It takes time and support for teachers to learn to conduct classes in this way. Some of the changes are relatively easy (for example, asking students to explain the thinking behind their problem solutions), but learning to use the pedagogical approaches in the service of rigorous mathematical learning takes time for reflection, refinement, and practice.

[10] Excerpted from *Professional Standards for Teaching Mathematics*. (1991). Reston, VA: National Council of Teachers of Mathematics (pp. 53–54).

Implementing the pedagogical innovations of standards-based curricula does not mean simply adopting new forms of teaching in and of themselves. Standards-based instruction employs these forms of teaching in the service of promoting students' learning of important mathematical content. The purpose of asking students to share their thinking, for example, is not simply to have students participate in class discussion but to bring mathematical ideas to the attention of the class in order to explore and develop them further. However, simply sharing their thinking doesn't ensure that students will learn more mathematics. The teacher must *do* something with these ideas in order to promote further mathematical understanding—for example, pose a new problem, raise questions that cause students to extend their thinking, or have students with different ideas work together so they each have a chance to think about the subject in new ways.

Teachers also need personal and emotional support during implementation, although this is rarely acknowledged as an important part of the process. Standards-based curricula make a variety of new demands on teachers which may leave even the most experienced veterans feeling somewhat uncertain— even uneasy—about their mathematics teaching. It is difficult for people who take pride in their work and have a strong sense of responsibility as educators to feel suddenly less confident in their ability to implement the new materials. Some have suggested that the job of preparing to teach new content while developing new instructional techniques is much like trying to re-engineer an airplane while it's in the air. The end result may be vastly improved, but there are some harrowing moments along the way. It is important to be sensitive to these issues when providing support to teachers and address them as directly as you can.

Meeting Ongoing Implementation Needs

Teachers who are working to deepen and extend their classroom practice are engaged in serious and substantial professional development. Your support of their efforts is an investment in the quality of your community's teaching and learning. You can support their ongoing implementation needs in a number of ways. Some strategies that other districts have used are described below.

- Develop workshops, seminars, and summer institutes focusing on instructional issues that are particularly germane to your faculty. Examples of issues that have been relevant to districts include exploring new mathematical content from the curriculum, developing assessment tools, and analyzing student work.

- Provide teachers with information about opportunities for ongoing professional development. Contact local university partners and educational organizations for their course offerings; get referrals for seminars, workshops, and institutes from the NCTM and the NSF-funded implementation centers; and use the World Wide Web to find professional development courses (see "Professional Development Resources" at the end of this section for some specific websites).

• Continue holding grade-level meetings at which the focus is on substantive issues of mathematics learning and teaching. Hold cross-grade meetings on a regular basis, as well, so that teachers can develop a broader perspective on the curriculum as a whole and the development of mathematical ideas throughout the grade span.

• Provide mentors to consult with teachers about their practice. Mentors can help teachers with implementation issues in a number of ways, for example, observing lessons and debriefing with the teacher afterward, coaching, demonstrating lessons, co-teaching, and providing assistance in planning lessons.

• Encourage teachers and principals to develop a culture of inquiry in their schools in order to promote a work environment that encourages reflection and thoughtful discussion among colleagues. While there's no recipe for developing this kind of atmosphere, there are some qualities that can help, such as administrators' interest in participating in substantive conversations about mathematics and mathematics teaching; respect among the faculty for teachers' efforts to change their practice; the ability to listen to colleagues without evaluating them; and a willingness to try out new ideas.

• Help teachers develop skills and strategies for serving as spokespeople. Parents often call on their children's teachers to represent the new curriculum. All members of the school community should be prepared to educate parents about the changes happening in mathematics education within the district.

• Provide training for principals and mathematics department heads about the philosophy and goals of mathematics education reform and the particular instructional demands of the curriculum you have just adopted. In addition to serving as instructional leaders for the teaching staff, these administrators must be able to represent the new programs to parents and be prepared to listen to parents' concerns.

• Provide written support material to teachers. Some resources and sources for further information are included below.

Professional Development Resources

Selected Print and Video Materials

Professional Development Materials

- **Bridges to Classroom Mathematics** (publisher: COMAP) is designed for elementary school teachers. It includes a generic professional development component that is appropriate for use with teachers implementing any standards-based curriculum, and components specific to *Everyday Mathematics* and *Investigations in Number, Data and Space*. Find more information at the COMAP website <http://www.comap.com/elem_bridges_to_classroom_mathematics.htm> or call (800) 772-6627.

- **Developing Mathematical Ideas** (publisher: Cuisenaire • Dale Seymour) is available as a series of modules focusing on students' development of particular mathematical ideas central to the elementary grades curriculum. It is appropriate for teachers working with any standards-based curriculum. Contact Cuisenaire • Dale Seymour at (800) 872-1100.

- **STREAM** (publisher: COMAP) is a collection of video and print materials designed to provide an introduction to important themes of mathematics education at the secondary level. These materials are intended for use with teachers, parents, and administrators. Find more information at <http://www.comap.com/hs_secondary_training_reform_materials.htm> or call (800) 772-6627.

- The **Annenberg/CPB (Corporation for Public Broadcasting) Learner Online Math and Science Collection** contains print guides, videos, and software showing concrete examples of good teaching and active learning in a variety of settings. It also includes professional development resources for teachers. More information is available at <http://www.learner.org/collections/mathsci/>.

- The **TIMSS (Third International Mathematics and Science Study) Resource Kit**, available through the National Council of Teachers of Mathematics (NCTM), contains four modules designed to foster examination of curriculum, teaching, student achievement, and pursuing excellence in education. The kit also includes understandable reports of TIMSS research findings; videotapes of classroom teaching; guides for using the research information in discussions; presentation overheads with talking points for speakers; checklists, leaflets, and flyers. For more information, call (800) 235-7566 or visit the NCTM website at <http://www.nctm.org/catalog/new-resources/668.html>.

Resources for Designing and Developing Professional Development Programs

Many currently available print resources and videotapes can be used to provide examples of standards-based instruction and stimulate discussion in professional development settings. In addition to the resources listed below, contact the publisher of your curriculum and the appropriate satellite implementation center about the availability of materials specific to the curriculum you have adopted.

- **Ideas at Work: Mathematics Professional Development** is a pamphlet published by the Eisenhower National Clearinghouse for Mathematics and Science Education. It presents a framework for creating professional development programs and summarizes different strategies for professional development. Contact the Clearinghouse at (800) 621-5785 or on the web at <http://www.enc.org>.

- **Designing Professional Development for Teachers of Science and Mathematics** by Susan Loucks-Horsley, Peter W. Hewson, Nancy Love, and Katherine E. Stiles (Thousand Oaks, CA: Corwin Press, 1998) offers an in-depth examination of the principles of effective professional development and a discussion of the issues that emerge in applying those principles in practice. This book would be an excellent resource for those interested in an expanded treatment of the ideas suggested in *Ideas at Work*.

Case Materials

Several casebooks address the issues involved in learning to use standards-based mathematics materials, including:

- *Fractions, Decimals, Ratios and Percents: Hard to Teach and Hard to Learn?* by Carne Barnett. (Portsmouth, N.H.: Heinemann, 1994)

- *Windows on Teaching: Cases of Secondary Mathematics Classrooms* by the Harvard Mathematics Case Development Project. For information contact the Harvard Project on Schooling and Children at 126 Mount Auburn Street, Cambridge, MA 02138, or call (617) 496-6883.

- *Reconstructing Mathematics Education: Stories of Teachers Meeting the Challenge of Reform* by Deborah Schifter & Catherine Twomey Fosnot. (New York: Teachers College Press, 1993)

- *What's Happening in Math Class? Volume 1: Envisioning New Practices through Teacher Narratives,* edited by Deborah Schifter. (New York: Teachers College Press, 1996)

- *What's Happening in Math Class? Volume 2: Reconstructing Professional Identities,* edited by Deborah Schifter. (New York: Teachers College Press, 1996)

Professional Development Contacts

- Publishers offer some introductory professional development. Contact the publisher of the curriculum you have adopted to find out about its workshops.

- NSF implementation centers have professional development offerings. Contact information for the implementation centers is provided in Appendices 1 and 2.

- A number of organizations have information on their websites regarding professional development in mathematics. Some also have up-to-date databases that list professional development programs. Here are some examples:

~ National Science Foundation, <http://www.nsf.gov>. The Teacher Enhancement Program in NSF's Division of Elementary, Secondary, and Informal Science Education funds Local Systemic Change projects and Educational Leadership projects. See <http://www.ehr.nsf.gov/EHR/ESIE/programs.htm>.

~ U.S. Department of Education <http://www.ed.gov>. The Eisenhower National Clearinghouse (ENC) is a resource for K-12 mathematics and science educators which is funded through a contract with the U.S. Department of Education. ENC provides a searchable database for information on education-related issues. See <http://www.enc.org>. ENC also provides professional development links that highlight strategies and successful programs across the country at <http://www.enc.org/reform/ideas/133273/index.htm>.

~ TERC <http://www.terc.edu> is a nonprofit, educational research organization that focuses on mathematics and science teaching and learning. At <http://www.terc.edu/getinvolved.html>, TERC lists workshops, field test results and research studies about mathematics education.

~ National Staff Development Council (NSDC) <http://www.nsdc.org>. The NSDC is a nonprofit organization providing services and publications about planning and implementing staff development. It offers an array of workshops and a training academy for staff developers.

~ National Council of Teachers of Mathematics (NCTM) <http://www.nctm.org>. NCTM posts online announcements and links for upcoming professional development opportunities. Workshops, conferences, and grants are among the informational categories. See <http://www.nctm.org/classifieds/announcements/index.html>.

~ Math Forum <http://www.forum.swarthmore.edu>. The Math Forum is an online community of math educators, researchers, and students that provides web-based discussions, interactive question services, and links to mathematics education sites. The Math Forum professional development link at <http://forum.swarthmore.edu/mathed/professional.dev.html> provides a list of internet resources for teacher education and development.

~ Project 2061, of the American Association for the Advancement of Science, offers several types of workshops which can be customized for the particular needs of a district or individual school. Learn more about these professional development programs at <http://project2061.aaas.org/pdp/wkshop.html>.

Budgeting for Professional Development

As we work and talk with district leaders who have been implementing standards-based mathematics programs, one message always comes through loud and clear: Teachers need support to learn how to implement standards-based curricula effectively, and this support costs money. There's really no other way to ensure a successful implementation. There are layers of complexity to the instructional approaches these curricula employ, and teachers cannot be expected to uncover and master them all without assistance. Without professional development for teachers, the success of your implementation will be at risk, so make sure that you plan for these costs in your budget (see Chapter 7, "Cost Considerations").

You can be creative about how to piggyback moneys to pay for this professional development. One district, for example, obtained a matching funds grant from its NSF-supported State Systemic Initiative (SSI) to buy teachers a free period to use as a common preparation time. Some districts have been successful in arranging for volunteers from local businesses and industries to serve as substitute teachers one day a month so teachers can attend professional development seminars.

Summary

Be strategic about your plans for teacher support. Your professional development will be a lot more effective if, at the outset, you anticipate your major needs and develop focused plans for allocating resources to address them. (This was one of the major reasons you conducted the needs and resources assessment detailed in Chapter 4.) There are two main issues to think about when planning your professional development: (1) providing ongoing teacher support, and (2) scaling up your implementation.

Remember that the implementation process for teachers who are new to standards-based mathematics materials is a rather extended one, and that teachers' needs change over time. Be prepared to offer teachers "just in time" support at the outset of the adoption and to shift to more substantive mathematical and pedagogical professional development as implementation progresses. Also, your professional development will have a greater impact on teachers' practice if you focus on a small number of critical challenges, rather than taking more of a smorgasbord approach.

In some districts (and at some grade levels) scaling up means that every teacher in the district is using the new curriculum materials; in others, a full-scale implementation does not necessarily mean that you will find the new curriculum on every desk in every classroom. Whatever full-scale implementation means for your own district, you will need to have a plan for responding to the professional development needs of an entire district of teachers who are at different points in the implementation process (see also Chapter 11, "Implementation Rollout").

CHAPTER 10

Community Support

When people talk about enlisting community support for mathematics curriculum adoption, what they are usually talking about is the need for *parent* support. There is no doubt that securing parent support for standards-based curricula is critical for a successful adoption. At the minimum, parents' concerns divert teachers' time and attention away from their focus on classroom instruction. When opposition is highly organized and forceful, it can seriously undermine a district's use of standards-based materials.

Because parent support is so crucial, it is the focus of this chapter. There is another aspect to building community support, which is to identify and cultivate those resources within your community that will help you facilitate the selection and implementation process. We include a brief discussion of community resources at the end of the chapter.

Building Parent Understanding and Support

Not long ago, a group of about 100 parents filed into a cavernous school auditorium to listen to a lecture by a noted mathematics educator and outspoken advocate of mathematics education reform. She sought to convey the ideas behind the mathematics reform movement to the parents by engaging them in problems requiring mathematical reasoning, sharing examples of students' work, and describing some of her own experiences as a classroom teacher and mathematics learner. When she opened the floor to the audience at the end of the evening, their questions and comments revealed the two fundamental concerns that parents were then (and are still) voicing all over the nation.

The first concern came from parents who were worried or skeptical about the new curricula. They wanted to know whether the changes in the approach to mathematics advocated by standards-based reform will compromise children's opportunities to learn the "important math" they need for future success. (What constitutes the "important math" is not exactly clear. Often, it bears a strong resemblance to the mathematics that the parents, themselves, learned in school.) While the parents seemed to appreciate the lecturer's examples of students successfully solving mathematical problems (many of which involved demonstrations of computational ingenuity), one evening's worth of interesting anecdotes doesn't necessarily provide enough information to reassure parents that this new approach to mathematics is educationally sound, or that it will benefit their own children.

The second concern was voiced by parents who were looking for ways to help their children with mathematics. These parents found the work their children were bringing home to be completely unfamiliar, even baffling—unlike any mathematics that they knew or understood from their own schooling. This lack of connection left them feeling unable to play an active role in supporting their children's mathematical learning. These parents wanted assistance in becoming resources. They wanted to know how they could learn enough about the mathematics their children were studying to be able to provide assistance and encouragement at home. Some parents also very tentatively expressed a concern about the adequacy of their own mathematical understanding and anxiety about the possibility that they would not, in fact, be able to provide this assistance.

None of the concerns expressed that evening were unusual or unexpected. You will need to address both of these kinds of concerns during the course of your adoption process if you are to have good working relationships with the parents in your district. Below we offer some of the methods districts have developed to inform parents about new mathematics programs and build their support for those programs.

Increasing Parents' Awareness and Understanding

Meetings

Meetings are an effective way to reach groups of parents to inform them about standards-based curricula. It's important to help parents understand why the district is considering these curricula, give them a sense of what the curricula are like, and reassure them that the district is making sound educational decisions. Parents need an opportunity to get this information, and they also need a forum to air their concerns. Districts commonly hold all or some of the following kinds of meetings over the course of the adoption process: informational meetings, curriculum nights, and math nights.

Informational Meetings for the Community

If your district is just beginning to consider standards-based curricula, hold general information meetings to orient parents to the goals and visions of mathematics education reform. Make sure that participants include teachers from the district who are respected by parents, are familiar with the new curricula (and mathematics education reform in general), and can be articulate spokespeople for the new programs. Some districts hold meetings during the selection process in order to keep the community apprised of the curricula that are under consideration. Focus these meetings on the distinctions between different potential candidates and give parents a sense of how the programs would help the district achieve its goals for mathematics education. If you have a community cable TV station, consider broadcasting these meetings to reach more people.

Describe the NCTM *Standards* and the philosophy behind them, and review your district's standards and goals for mathematics education. Be ready to address parents' concerns that the new curricula may not prepare their children adequately. Most publishers have student performance data that you can share with parents to obviate some of these concerns. Part of the purpose of these meetings should also be to help parents begin to reconsider the kinds of skills and understanding that are part of a strong mathematical education. You can give parents a sense of the kind of work and thinking that standards-based curricula seek to promote by showing video clips of classroom lessons. (See the highlighted section on "Professional Development Resources" in Chapter 9, "Teacher Support" for video resources you can use with parents.)

If you are already implementing a standards-based curriculum at another grade level, consider inviting students from some of these classes to talk about their experiences and share some of their work. Students are often among the most compelling advocates for these curricula.

It is very important to provide time to listen carefully to those who have come to the meeting. Some parents will attend just to hear what the district's plans are, others will have questions, and still others will express concerns. Remember that parents and district staff both want students to succeed in mathematics. Parents' beliefs about the ways to achieve that success come largely from their own experiences as mathematics students (which are almost never based in the kinds of approaches used in the current standards-based programs). Many of their concerns are expressions of uncertainty about the effectiveness of approaches that are unfamiliar. Meetings offer an important venue for parents' concerns to be raised and acknowledged, and they provide district personnel with information about the kinds of issues they must continue to address.

Curriculum Nights

Many schools hold curriculum nights early in the school year to introduce parents to their children's teachers and to describe the current year's curriculum. These provide an opportunity to give parents a brief overview of the new mathematics curriculum once it has been adopted.

Describe the mathematical goals of the curriculum, and how it is similar to and different from earlier mathematics programs. Explain the philosophy behind the changes in content and pedagogical approach, giving concrete examples from students' work wherever possible. Sometimes it is helpful for parents to see connections between the changes proposed for mathematics and similar kinds of changes in other content areas.

Math Nights

Many schools are beginning to institute math nights, where parents and other family members can spend an evening exploring some of the mathematics from the new curriculum. These evenings can offer parents a more detailed picture of the curriculum the district has adopted (or is considering). Some schools hold one math night a year as a general introduction for parents to standards-based mathematics. Others hold these meetings for each grade on a regular basis throughout the year, to introduce parents to their children's units of study.

The evenings are generally organized around a mathematics activity. Working through an activity offers parents firsthand experience with the kind of mathematical thinking that teachers are striving to achieve in their classrooms. It gives them a better sense of how the lessons are run and how the curriculum engages students' thinking and promotes understanding. This, in turn, can help make the curriculum feel more accessible and give parents a better sense of how to help their children with homework. Finally, math nights can open up more opportunities for communication between parents, teachers, and students.

On Doing Mathematics with Parents

One of the best ways to give people a sense of the kind of mathematical thinking promoted by standards-based curricula is to have them work on mathematics problems. Doing mathematics helps make abstract talk about goals and pedagogies seem more concrete. It gives parents a chance to experience firsthand some opportunities for mathematical reasoning, and may actually help build their confidence in their own mathematical thinking. Doing mathematics also gives parents a chance to see how the curriculum develops certain mathematical ideas.

When you plan mathematical activities for parents, choose a sample activity from the new curriculum that you can do together in 15 or 20 minutes. To minimize potential discomfort and maximize parent engagement, make sure that you choose an exploration that relies on mathematical ideas that are familiar to your audience. (Don't, however, presume that everyone will be able to successfully reach a solution.) If one of your goals is to have people share ideas with one another, be prepared to facilitate this process, as most adults are unaccustomed to working together on mathematics.

A Note of Caution

Be aware that "going public" with mathematics is often uncomfortable for those who are uncertain of their own mathematical abilities. Some parents may find working on mathematics problems to be unsettling. When working with parents,

DO:

- Choose problems illustrating the mathematical point(s) you want to make that will be familiar and accessible to your audience.

- Acknowledge the ideas that participants bring to the activity.

- Discuss the mathematical ideas behind the activity, and the learning that builds on these ideas.

DON'T:

- Assume (or convey the assumption) that the mathematics will necessarily be easy or obvious to those working on the problem.

- Assume that everyone will feel comfortable volunteering ideas in a mathematics discussion.

If you need help finding an activity that is both engaging and illustrative of the mathematical thinking you are seeking for your students, get advice from others. Check with colleagues who have held successful parent meetings of their own, consult with the publisher (some of the activities they use in informational presentations may be appropriate) or the curriculum developers, or contact the appropriate satellite implementation center(s) for advice about framing the activity so that it connects to the broader mathematical agenda of the curriculum (see Appendix 2 for satellite implementation center contact information). Also, make sure that you select mathematically sophisticated and experienced facilitators to conduct these math nights.

Local News Media

Districts can be strategic about using newspapers, radio, and school newsletters to carry stories about mathematics education reform, new curriculum possibilities, and students' classroom activities. The media can also serve as a way to keep community members updated about adoption efforts within the district and can provide a forum for dialogue about district plans.

Parent Handbooks

Some districts have found it useful to create handbooks to orient parents to the philosophy and goals of standards-based curricula. Include a description of the program, examples of the kinds of mathematical ideas the students will be studying, and examples of mathematical problems. Use sections from the teacher's guide (or companion implementation guides that many curricula have developed) to help you frame the context of such a handbook. If you can find examples of student work that illustrate mathematical reasoning at different grade levels, include these as well. Use examples from your own students whenever possible— they're more compelling than those from anonymous children. You can also look for examples of student work in the curriculum's teacher's guide.

Course Descriptions

Parents will feel more comfortable with their children's mathematics classes when they have a sense that their children are learning the "important math." One simple way to provide some reassurance is to identify courses (particularly at the high school level) in ways that are familiar to parents. When courses bear unfamiliar names or descriptions, parents may feel less confident about the effectiveness of the curricula. Taking time to craft course descriptions that make connections to the important areas traditionally covered in mathematics texts will go a long way toward alleviating parents' concerns.

Helping Parents Become More Supportive and Knowledgeable Resources for Their Children

Parents want to be able to help their children with their school work, but many parents find the mathematics in standards-based curricula to be unfamiliar and often inaccessible. They don't understand what their children are doing and don't know how to help. Below are some suggestions for ways to help parents learn more about the district's mathematics programs and become better resources for their children.

Homework

Homework serves a dual function: It supports and extends students' classroom work, and it serves as parents' most consistent and prominent connection to their children's mathematics education. Because parents' images of mathematics lessons are largely shaped by the work their children bring home, encourage teachers to think about homework assignments from a parent's perspective. One administrator noted that the teachers in her district screened homework assignments from their new curriculum, only sending work home that would look familiar and comprehensible to the students' parents. Others take the perspective that homework offers parents an excellent chance to think more deeply about mathematical ideas with their children. Parents may be eager to help their children with their homework but may need some guidance from teachers on how to go about it.

Letters to Parents

Many curricula include sample letters to parents in the teacher's guide to help facilitate communication between school and home. Teachers can keep parents apprised of their children's work and the content they are studying through occasional letters home. These can describe students' work in class and relate it to the major mathematical ideas of the unit. Some curricula, particularly at the elementary school level, include sample letters to parents. If teachers will be writing letters of their own, they can base the letters on the unit introduction from the teacher's guide. Letters home can offer tips to parents for helping their children with upcoming homework.

Consultants

Your district can hire outside consultants from local universities or other educational agencies to work with parents on an occasional basis. For example, one district hired a local mathematics educator to offer a series of evening lectures about mathematics education. Another hired a full-time consultant for the first year of the adoption to answer parents' questions and support teachers' implementation efforts. Parents appreciated the fact that someone in the district was serving as an ombudsman, and teachers not only got help with the particulars of classroom implementation but were relieved of some of the responsibility of addressing parents' concerns. The consultant's joint responsibilities allowed her to integrate the needs and concerns of both teachers and parents while working to facilitate the implementation of the curriculum.

Courses for Parents

Some districts offer evening or Saturday courses for parents, designed to help them understand more about mathematics education reform in general and the mathematics their children are studying through the new curriculum in particular. These courses are generally designed to allow parents to explore mathematical ideas covered by the curriculum, using similar pedagogical approaches. These courses can vary in length, from three or four sessions to as many as six or eight.

We have Saturday morning programs for seventh and eighth grade students in math and science, which include separate sessions for parents. They have to come to the first session in order for their children to attend, and more and more parents are coming to every session. These are opportunities for parents to be exposed to the new ways their kids are learning math. (J.C., mathematics supervisor)

Websites

There are a number of websites parents can visit that present standards-based perspectives on mathematics education, pose interesting mathematical problems and solutions, offer online forums and discussions, and list other resources and contacts. Good sites to check include the following:

- The Math Forum website includes a "For Concerned Parents and Citizens" page at <http://forum.swarthmore.edu/parents.citizens.html>.

- The Eisenhower National Clearinghouse website offers many professional development resources, but also contains articles and activities that can be helpful for parents; see <http://www.enc.org>.

- The PBS Mathline at <http://www.pbs.org/mathline>, primarily a resource for teachers, also can help acquaint parents with standards-based mathematics.

- The National Council of Teachers of Mathematics (NCTM) website publishes articles and information that may help parents become more familiar with issues related to standards-based mathematics; see <http://www.nctm.org>.

- The Annenberg/CPB Learner Online Math and Science Collection at <http://www.learner.org/collections/mathsci/> also contains a "Working with Parents" section that provides activities for parents and children, as well as materials to help schools and parents discuss mathematics education reform.

As you search the Internet for information about mathematics education reform, you may discover a number of sites with decidedly anti-reform messages. You may want to visit these (it's likely that some of the parents in your community will be doing so) to learn about their perspectives. This will help prepare you in case you are called on to address their arguments in your own district.

Using Community Resources

Take advantage of the expertise within your community to support your adoption effort. The needs and resources assessment you conducted during the selection phase will have identified some of the people who can help you. Below are some suggestions for ways to take advantage of the resources in your own district:

- Invite parents and other community members who use mathematics in their work (or their recreation) to talk with students.

- Create release time for teachers' professional development by arranging for local businesses and industries to volunteer staff as substitute teachers. (This model has been used with considerable success in some districts.)[11]

- Arrange with the business community for jobs and/or internships for students interested in firsthand experience with mathematics-related work.

- Call on university partners or other educational institutions to consult on the design and delivery of professional development for teachers.

---

[11] For a handbook describing the industry volunteer model, see *The Industry Volunteer Handbook* produced by the Industry Volunteers in the Classroom project at Education Development Center, Inc., in Newton, MA. (Ordering information is available by calling 800-793-5076 or on the web at <http://www.edc.org/LTT/IVM>.)

CHAPTER 11

Implementation Rollout

There are a number of options for achieving full-scale implementation of your new curriculum. In this chapter we discuss the various ways in which districts have moved from early implementation to districtwide use of a new curriculum.

Some districts choose to implement a new curriculum program districtwide in order to effect coordinated, systemic change in the district. This strategy can serve as an opportunity to focus energies and coordinate resources across the district and the community, engaging the efforts of teachers, students, and parents to improve mathematics learning. It also allows the district to design a coherent plan for professional development and support that is centered on helping teachers throughout the district implement the standards-based curriculum.

> *[Our district] is shooting for large-scale buy-in, a long implementation process where teachers teach teachers and get a lot of support. (E.B., mathematics curriculum supervisor)*

Choosing to adopt a new curriculum districtwide does not necessarily mean that you will implement it all at once. In fact, this "whole hog" approach is a rather uncommon strategy. Most districts plan to phase in their new curriculum—often over several years—building the community support and teacher expertise needed to carry the implementation forward.

When planning your implementation strategy, you should consider the following questions:

- **What are your goals for "full implementation"?** Think about what you want full implementation to look like in your district. Do you want every teacher and student districtwide to use the new program? Do you want to strive for partial implementation, i.e., a majority of teachers and students in the district use the new curriculum but some students and teachers remain with the current program? For some districts, having every teacher in every school using the new curriculum may be an unrealistic initial implementation goal, particularly at the high school level, where the pressures of high-stakes testing often mitigate against a single program for all students. Some districts choose to offer two or even three curricular options for high school students, especially during early implementation, when there is little information about how the new curriculum will affect student performance. Collecting data about students' learning during the implementation process will help you answer questions like these and adapt your implementation plan as you go along.

- **Does your implementation strategy provide sufficient time and teacher support as you scale up the implementation?** Moving to full implementation is fundamentally an issue of scale, particularly for large districts with many teachers. As with any innovation, implementing a new curriculum on a large scale will probably turn out to be harder and take longer than you originally thought. This is especially true if a large number of teachers will need significant amounts of professional development and support to learn to use the new curriculum effectively. Since districts may not have the resources and structure to provide adequate support to every teacher at once, many districts choose to take a more gradual approach to implementation, working with smaller groups of teachers through a more extended implementation process.

- **What implementation strategy is best suited to the particular curriculum you have chosen?** The philosophy and design of the particular curriculum you have selected may influence your choice of strategy. Consult the publishers and developers of the program you have selected about implementation; they may have suggestions about particular strategies that have been effective when implementing their programs. For example, in a program that tightly develops a particular mathematical idea across the grades, certain ideas may be dependent on other ideas or skills that are developed in earlier grades or may themselves be prerequisites for work in later grades. The developers may strongly recommend a grade-by-grade implementation approach for this curriculum so that students will be appropriately prepared for each subsequent grade level.

These questions will help you identify major implementation goals and constraints. Keep them in mind as you consider the following rollout strategies.

Adoption by Certain Schools

One implementation strategy is to introduce a new curriculum in one or two schools and then extend the implementation to more schools over time. This strategy has the advantage of building both grassroots interest in the curriculum and a cadre of experienced teachers who can serve as resources to their colleagues in other schools.

Four or five schools decided to go ahead with the new program for kindergarten and grade 1. Some people were ready, and some didn't agree with the decision yet; teachers have a lot of autonomy in our town. A good number of teachers are used to being able to write their own materials. Our process gave them time to really get behind this adoption. Since we started with five schools, we always had some schools that acted as lead schools, where teachers from one of the other ten schools could go and observe. (M.T., K–8 mathematics coordinator)

The school-by-school adoption approach also allows for the development of a supportive culture for the implementation within each school. Much of the day-to-day work of teaching with the new materials is hammered out within the individual schools. This is where teachers can discuss their lessons, ask questions about the curriculum, and share implementation ideas with colleagues in the lunch room, after school, or during preparation periods. In addition, this strategy gives the district additional time to prepare teachers in schools that are slated for later phases of the adoption, providing the training and professional development they need before taking on a standards-based program. One drawback of this approach is that new materials and teaching practices take a longer time to spread throughout the district.

If you decide to adopt a school-by-school strategy, recognize that you may need to find a way to maintain interest and commitment within each school across the district as you roll out the implementation. Since teachers often are more receptive to working with the new curriculum when an interest in the materials develops from inside the schools rather than coming from above, you should capitalize on the enthusiasm of teachers already using the curriculum to help move the implementation process forward.

Adoption by One Grade Level at a Time

Another implementation option is to phase in the new curriculum one grade level at a time. This method has the advantage of creating a core of teachers who can support other teachers who are new to the program. These teacher leaders can serve as mentors, providing practical and personal support for their colleagues. This strategy also enables the district to provide intensive training and professional development for teachers at each grade level. One district, for example, offered monthly training sessions for all teachers during the first three years of implementation. In addition, each school was assigned a mentor teacher who was on part-time (paid) leave from the classroom to support the implementation. One disadvantage of this grade-by-grade method is that the students who begin the program in the first year of implementation will always have teachers who are teaching with new materials for the first time.

The particular curriculum you have adopted may recommend a specific strategy for implementation. The grade-by-grade implementation, for example, is favored by programs in which the mathematics activities in one grade are dependent on specific activities that are part of the previous year's curriculum.

One district phased in a middle school curriculum by having all of the sixth grade teachers and a core group of seventh grade volunteers teach the program in the first year. The seventh grade volunteers were then in a position to take leadership roles with their colleagues the following year, when all seventh grade teachers began using the curriculum. In the second year the implementation model also broadened to include eighth grade volunteers. These eighth grade teachers gained experience with the curriculum that they could then share with their colleagues during the full eighth grade implementation in the third year.

YEAR 1	YEAR 2	YEAR 3
All 6th grade teachers, plus volunteers at grade 7.	Remaining 7th grade teachers, plus volunteers at grade 8.	Remaining 8th grade teachers.
Grade 6		
	Grade 7	
		Grade 8

The grade-by-grade strategy builds on teachers' experience and interest and encourages teachers at each grade level to work with their colleagues. However, if teachers do not have the appropriate support or if teacher leadership is weak at certain grade levels, the implementation may experience more difficulties or delays.

Adoption by a Cluster of Grade Levels

A variant of the grade-by-grade strategy is to introduce a new program at clusters of grade levels. This is particularly common in the elementary grades, where rolling out a new program grade by grade over six or seven grade levels would take several years. Thus, for example, a district may decide to phase in the new curriculum in all K–2 classes during the first year of implementation and to add grades 3–5 in the second. Implementation by clusters of grade levels enables a quicker implementation, but one that is still gradual enough to allow districts to provide professional development and support to a manageable number of teachers.

In addition to reducing the burden on initial professional development demands, this strategy can help accommodate potential overlaps or gaps in content across the grade levels. As the new curriculum may introduce mathematical skills and concepts in a slightly different order and at somewhat different grade levels than past programs (for example, focusing on addition of fractions with unlike denominators in sixth grade instead of fifth), it is somewhat easier to coordinate the content among grade levels if the curriculum is adopted within grade clusters. Teachers then can work together across grades to minimize discontinuity for students. With this method, implementation seems to be most challenging in the later grades of the grade-level cluster. For example, one district adopting in grades 3–5 concurrently had the hardest time at the fifth grade because students had to catch up with new material that they would have learned in fourth grade, had they started the program at the beginning and worked straight through. One way to address this issue is to consider using a "grade-by-grade/grade cluster" hybrid strategy. Begin implementation with a single grade in different grade clusters (e.g., start with kindergarten and with grade 3), and add subsequent grades in the following years (e.g., add grades 1 and 4 in the second year of implementation, and grades 2 and 5 in the third year). If you consider implementing within clusters of grades, look carefully grade by grade for possible gaps between the existing program and the new curriculum.

Adoption by Certain Classes or Certain Students

Districts may chose to introduce a curriculum slowly by adopting the mathematics program for certain classes or certain students at a particular grade level. This is most common at the upper grades where there is more pressure to track and accelerate certain students. One rationale for this approach is to provide students and teachers with some choice of curricula. One district, for example, began a new high school curriculum in selected ninth grade classes, but some parents complained that the program did not allow enough flexibility of choice for those students who could move through it more quickly. As a result, the school developed an accelerated option for the course in the second year of implementation. Another district introduced a new program for students who were not succeeding in the existing program. Although these students learned a lot and began to make up some of their lost ground, the curriculum became identified as a remedial one and the district had a hard time convincing other parents that the program was appropriate for students at all achievement levels.

> *[The recently chosen standards-based program] isn't a schoolwide adoption and, given our system, probably nothing would be. We have the advanced placement track that looks like it'll remain the same, and then we have the basic, standard, and honors levels. Twenty-five percent of the students are taking [the new curriculum], and we'll probably cap it there. One-half of the teachers are trained to teach [the program], and our goal is to get 80 percent of the teachers trained. . . I wouldn't force any teacher to participate. All our teachers have volunteered, and no student was forced to take it. We'd already made [these implementation] mistakes [in the past]. (M.N., high school teacher leader)*

Although some districts have found it best to offer standards-based classes as an alternative to their traditional mathematics curriculum, others have been able to move from using the new curriculum with certain groups of students to using it with virtually all of the students in the school. For example, one high school phased in a standards-based curriculum over a three-year period. They began in the first year with those ninth grade students who were performing in the bottom half of the class in mathematics. In the second year, the original group continued with the second year of the program, and students who had been unsuccessful in the traditional course the previous year were moved into the standards-based program, either repeating ninth grade mathematics with the standards-based program or joining their classmates in the second year of the new curriculum, depending on the extent and degree of the difficulties they had encountered. In the third year of implementation, all incoming ninth graders used the standards-based curriculum. A small group of entering ninth graders who were exceptional mathematics students were accelerated into the second year of the curriculum, taking their mathematics classes with tenth graders.

> *The parents don't see the math in the reform curricula, and we wondered whether it made sense to continue a traditional track and have [the new high school curriculum]. We decided not to because we worried that [the new curriculum] would become the low track. We don't know what's going to happen long-term. (J.F., K–12 mathematics supervisor)*

Adoption by Certain Teachers

Sometimes a group of teachers within a school or district leads the implementation. Expanding this group over time is a way to involve more teachers in using the new curriculum.

This strategy may be coupled with a grade-by-grade approach, with certain teachers at one grade implementing in advance of the full year implementation by all teachers at that grade level. In fact, any gradual implementation approach starts with a group of teachers who lead the charge. Districts frequently draw on the experience and expertise of these teachers in furthering the districtwide implementation of the program. These lead teachers may play a mentoring or coaching role for other teachers, they may demonstrate activities in other teachers' classrooms, and they often are called on to design and lead professional development for their colleagues.

One reason that districts take this approach is that it allows them to limit the amount of teacher support and professional development required for any given year. For example, one district that used a multi-year implementation model was able to provide teachers using the new program with valuable intensive support in the form of common planning time and team teaching opportunities, because they only needed to help a portion of their teaching staff each year. It is difficult—in fact, in large districts it is impossible—to provide the necessary professional development for teachers all at once. It is wiser to phase in your implementation so that you can offer teachers the support they need to use the curriculum effectively than it is to aim for a rapid, full-scale implementation that fails to meet teachers' and students' needs.

Beginning Your Adoption with Replacement Units

Districts may also use a replacement unit strategy to introduce new curricula in their schools. Because many of the new standards-based materials are modular, it is possible for teachers to try out one or two self-contained units without having to sustain big changes in their practice for the entire year. This gives teachers an opportunity to learn more about a new curriculum's approach and philosophy and to assess how the materials help to promote student learning. In some cases, replacement units are used as a selection as well as an implementation strategy. In others, replacement units are a way to begin the implementation process. Teachers at each grade implement part of the program during the first year and add more units in successive years.

A replacement unit strategy has the advantage of slowing down the transition for teachers. They can take the time they need to become accustomed to the new content and pedagogical techniques, and the district is able to gear staff development to the replacement units as part of the implementation process. Frequently, districts will select replacement units with some organizing theme or idea to afford a common experience and foster discussion among teachers.

The approach in one district was to choose one number unit, one geometry unit, and one computation unit at each grade level. Since teachers in each grade level were using new units with related content, there were many opportunities for cross-grades discussion. Another district chose to focus on algorithms and algebraic thinking, coordinating their professional development around this theme. Yet another district chose a common set of units so that they could monitor teachers' progress through each unit. Using a bi-weekly progress report, the district was able to collect valuable data on pacing, support needs, and challenges for teachers.

One potential disadvantage of this method is that students may experience inconsistencies between the existing program and the new units, especially if the structure and pedagogy of the two are very different. Sometimes teachers report bringing some of the instructional strategies they are learning to use with the standards-based units back to their other program, thereby reducing potential discontinuity in students' classroom learning experiences.

Full Implementation in One Year

Occasionally, districts will attempt full implementation in a single year. This approach is very challenging to undertake. The district must simultaneously attend to the many aspects of the change process—teacher support and professional development, community support, and assessment—across the district and still make sure that their students are engaging in high quality work. Most districts find that it is easier, more effective, and more sensible to take a slower, more gradual approach.

If I could do that over, I'd insist that it all be done in one year, because we have teacher mobility as well as student mobility. Also, when the focus is on your content area you have to jump on it and use your chance. (V.M., supervisor of mathematics, science, and technology)

Nonetheless, some districts do take this approach. Some feel that a shorter formal implementation phase maintains the momentum of the selection process. In some cases, your process for implementing new materials may be influenced by a timeline other than your own. Perhaps your district has money to support professional development for the new curriculum for only one year, or your policy or union rules dictate a certain timeline. District leadership can be creative about working around such conditions. For example, some districts have bought new materials according to the district budget cycle, but then held off on full implementation until they could provide the essential professional development for their staff.

Summary

There are a number of different, yet effective, strategies for rolling out the implementation of a new curriculum. Virtually all of these methods involve a multi-year plan that takes two to four years, and sometimes as many as six. Keep in mind that the implementation of any new curriculum, but particularly a standards-based program, is a complex and time-consuming process. Because these standards-based programs will demand changes in both content and instructional approaches for most teachers, you must be prepared to take the implementation slowly. The process will require preparation, planning, monitoring, and adaptation.

Many districts that have successfully adopted new materials deliberately began their teachers' professional development before the teachers were expected to use the new curriculum. This preparation period allowed teachers to begin to use the new materials with a sense of familiarity and an understanding of how to use them effectively. We encourage you to design your professional development plans accordingly.

Finally, we want to stress that there is no one correct implementation strategy. You must review the pros and cons of the various strategies presented here with an eye to your own circumstances, consult with others who have been involved with a recent implementation, and then craft an approach that will respond to the particulars of your situation. Make sure you consider your district's goals, your community, the size of your district, teachers' readiness, your available resources, and your timeline. By all means, consult with publishers and developers of the curriculum program (or programs) your district has selected. They may be able to recommend particular implementation models that are appropriate to their particular curriculum and direct you to people in other districts who can serve as resources. The NSF-funded implementation centers (listed in Appendices 1 and 2) also may have ideas about resources to help support your planning.

CHAPTER 12

Collecting Data about Implementation

Once your implementation is underway, you will want to know how it is going—how teachers are faring with the new program and how well your students are learning the mathematical ideas and skills specified by your state, district, and local standards. When implementation is an extended process (as it most often is with standards-based curricula) and you are savvy about collecting data as you monitor the implementation, you can keep the process on track by using the data to guide the adjustments and modifications you will need to make. Although not all districts take a systematic approach to gathering information about program implementation, it is not difficult to do and it provides a useful perspective on the adoption process. When you can base evaluations of your implementation on systematically collected data, you can be more confident of your conclusions and can make more informed adjustments to your implementation plans.

One focus of your data collection should be student learning and program implementation. In some sense districts are making a leap of faith about the value to students of adopting a standards-based curriculum. While these curricula are based on a firm grounding in educational psychology and mathematical development, as well as years of classroom-based experience with both the pedagogical approach and many of the mathematical lessons and activities, these programs in their current form are relatively new to the market. Because there is not yet a well-established track record for student performance for many of these curricula, you will need to monitor your students' learning closely to make sure that the district's goals are on track.

In addition to attending to student learning you should also collect data to help direct your program implementation, strategically identifying areas where teachers need further support. Guided by your data, you can capitalize on those aspects of the implementation that are working well and provide support for the challenges that confront teachers.

In this chapter we discuss collecting information about both of these areas: student learning and program implementation.

Collecting Information about Student Performance

Since the primary purpose of adopting a new mathematics curriculum is to benefit your students, you will obviously want to know how they are learning with the new curriculum. In fact, you will probably have several simultaneous agendas motivating your interest in student outcome data, including assessing student learning, monitoring and fine-tuning instruction, and addressing parents' requests for information about the effectiveness of the curriculum. Taking a close look at student performance can, for example, determine whether important skills or concepts are being sufficiently developed through your mathematics program or whether they need to be strengthened through lessons with supplementary materials.

Data about students' performance can appear in a variety of forms (e.g., tests, homework, class projects, and portfolios), which are all intended to reflect students' understanding of the material they are learning. In the daily course of classroom work, teachers need to know how students' understanding, skills, and attitudes are developing in order to fine-tune their instructional focus. It is also important to have a means for gauging students' progress, in terms of both their own growth and the district's standards.

Often, districts look first and foremost toward improvements in standardized test scores as evidence of a curriculum's effectiveness. These tests are powerful gatekeepers for future course placement and, as such, are particularly important to those who are invested in preparing students for college and subsequent career success. Yet there is significant ongoing debate among mathematics educators about whether these tests measure the kinds of mathematical reasoning and problem-solving abilities that have become the focus of mathematics education over the past decade. Many argue for better alignment of instruction and assessment, calling for the creation of new tests that will place more emphasis on reasoning and communication skills. Some of the recently developed state-level competency tests aim to do this by including open-ended problems that are scored with a rubric. (By aligning these tests with the kinds of thinking and learning promoted by standards-based curricula, designers and advocates of the new tests see them as levers for mathematics education reform.) Nonetheless, standardized tests remain a very real and significant presence in the educational landscape, and you are likely to confront the challenge of introducing new curricula and instructional approaches without losing ground on standardized test scores.

Interpreting Standardized Test Scores

Standardized tests, such as the California Achievement Test, the Illinois Test of Basic Skills, the SATs and the ACTs, are typically accorded great value within communities. For students, these tests are not only seen as measures of their current achievement and comparative standing, but as reliable projections of their overall aptitude and future educational promise. For districts, high test results are interpreted as an indicator of a quality educational system and low test results as a failure of both students and schools. Despite recent challenges to these assumptions, and questions about the alignment between the mathematics taught through the curriculum and that measured by the tests, standardized test results remain a central measure of success in many districts. A major goal in many communities is to maintain high scores or raise low ones. Few districts (if any) can introduce a new mathematics curriculum without considering its likely effect on test scores.

While standardized tests will not tell the whole story about your curriculum's success, they may represent the "bottom line" to the community—often, the effectiveness of the curriculum is equated with high (or rising) test scores. It is therefore important to help people interpret standardized test results so they can accord them appropriate importance and usefulness. Below are some points to keep in mind when looking to standardized tests for evidence of the success of any new curriculum.

Alignment of Curriculum and Assessment

Nationally normed tests (like the SATs) can give you an idea of how your district's students perform relative to other students, but they don't necessarily tell you about students' learning in terms of your own district's mathematics standards. Furthermore, students' standardized test scores will depend on the degree of alignment between the mathematical focus of the test and the curricular focus within your district. If there is little correspondence between the two, your students will be learning things that aren't covered by the test and the test will assess areas that students haven't learned. Under these circumstances, you should develop a plan for ensuring that your students will know the material covered by the test. You should also find other assessments (or develop ones of your own) that are better aligned with the content of your curriculum and your district's goals.

As you receive and interpret standardized test scores (and as you present them to the community), do so in the context of the question, "What is the correspondence between the areas assessed on the test and the areas emphasized by the curriculum we have adopted?" One way to answer this question is to analyze the test results in more detail. Instead of looking only at the overall test scores, concentrate on students' performance on those test items that best match the mathematics covered in your curriculum. (For example, look separately at performance on computational and conceptual subtests.) If the curriculum is effective in helping students develop into stronger mathematicians, you should see improvements on those items that best match with the curriculum content, even if the students' overall scores do not change appreciably.

Interpreting the Causes of Changing Test Scores

In general, current data from standards-based programs suggest that students' performance increases on conceptual components of tests and either remains the same or increases on the computational items. This pattern reflects the increased emphasis of the standards-based curricula on conceptual understanding. However, you should be prepared for the possibility that you will see little change in scores (or even some decrease in test results) during the first few years of implementation, as teachers and students learn to work with new mathematical ideas, classroom activities, and structures.

It is also important to add a caution here. While it is tempting to assume a cause-and-effect relationship between changing your mathematics program and changes in test scores (in either direction), it actually is difficult from a formal statistical standpoint to establish a direct causal connection. Even though it may *appear* that your introduction of a new curriculum is the reason that your students' test scores increase, proving that this is the case is actually rather difficult. For example, the increase in scores might be due to an overall increase in the amount of time teachers are spending doing mathematics during the course of the day, or students' increased engagement in their work. Most districts are happy enough with increases in test scores that they don't bother to try to isolate specific reasons for them beyond the observation that introducing a new curriculum coincided with the increase. If test results fail to improve, the tendency is to assume that the quality of the curriculum is at fault, when other factors that have only a secondary relationship to the curriculum, such as an incomplete or inadequately supported implementation, may be responsible.

Influence on Results of Students' Previous Mathematics Education

To the extent that a new curriculum does improve test scores by helping students get a better grasp of mathematical concepts, you might expect the effect to be strongest for elementary grade students who are just beginning their formal mathematics education. Middle and high school students whose previous instruction has not been as focused on developing mathematical reasoning and understanding may not show the same kinds of gains as younger students will. No matter how good a curriculum is, it cannot entirely remediate students' prior confusion or gaps in understanding, nor can it necessarily turn students who have been struggling with mathematics for years into confident and competent mathematicians.

Interpreting and Presenting Test Scores

We suggest that you use the following three approaches to interpret and present standardized test results in your district:

1. Pay attention to the alignment of assessment measures and your curriculum and instruction. When you collect data on standardized test performance and it is possible to do an item analysis of the tests, go the extra distance to do this analysis. Focus on students' changing performance on the items that match most closely with the areas covered in your curriculum, because these are where you should expect the greatest gains. When communicating with others in the community about test scores, talk specifically about student performance on these items.

2. Look for the biggest changes in the lower grade levels, where children are beginning their formal education with standards-based approaches. For example, compare previous scores of first and second grade classes (who used the old curriculum) with scores of first and second grade children learning with the new materials. (Recognize, however, that you are comparing different children who may have somewhat different mathematical abilities. When you make comparisons such as these, the assumption is that, on average, these students will be similar from year to year.) You can also look for changes in scores of the same children from years when they were using the old curriculum to years when they used the new one.

3. Don't expect significant changes for several years, as it will take at least that long for your program to be implemented fully and effectively. Until then, students may not receive the full benefit of the curriculum. In the meantime, pay attention to helping your teachers achieve "full implementation."

Collecting Information about Program Implementation

Because standards-based programs rely on pedagogical approaches that may be new to your teachers and involve new mathematical content as well, they will need time and support to learn to implement the program fully. It is useful, particularly in the first few years of implementing a standards-based curriculum, to gather information about how the process is going in order to help keep it on track. In districts that are currently using standards-based materials, implementation seems to have two phases. In the first year or two, teachers tend to focus on developing a feel for the curriculum, closely following the teacher's guide and building confidence in their grasp of the materials and the mathematical intent of the curriculum. During this early phase, many teachers are learning a new pedagogical approach to mathematics instruction and focusing their efforts on planning, pacing, and structuring lessons to promote students' mathematical exploration, reasoning, and problem solving. Teachers tend to focus on the structure and mechanics of the program, particularly if the pedagogical approach is new to them—how to use manipulatives, calculators, and computers; how to organize students into productive working groups; and how to manage a class discussion.

As teachers become more familiar and comfortable with the pedagogical and managerial demands of the program, they move to the second phase of implementation. In this phase, they begin to focus more on the mathematical content of the program and on ways to help their students develop deep and flexible understanding of the mathematics they are studying. You will see a shift in teachers' focus from the structure or pacing of lessons to using the program to promote students' mathematical thinking. Teachers begin to concentrate more on developing students' ideas, and begin to have questions about whether their interactions with students are stimulating deep thinking about mathematics. It is common, for example, for teachers to start to examine the kinds of questions they pose, the quality of the discussions they facilitate, or the decisions they are making about the mathematical focus of their classes.

> One indicator of successful implementation is the way teachers' expectations for professional development have changed. They are no longer equating professional development with the materials adoption cycle, but seeing it as more ongoing, where they can continue to focus on different issues important to them. (V.L.M., K–12 mathematics coordinator)

A major role for the implementation data you collect is to help plan professional development for your staff, matching the support you can provide to the aspects of the implementation that are most challenging to your teachers. One mathematics supervisor, during grade-level meetings focusing on implementation issues, collected short vignettes from teachers about dilemmas they encountered during implementation and some of the ways they dealt with them. She then used these vignettes with new teachers to raise issues and offer strategies to address them. Because the vignettes represented real situations that their colleagues had encountered and resolved, the teachers could both identify with the issues raised and feel encouraged that solutions were possible and practical.

Information about teachers' implementation of the curriculum will also help you interpret student outcome data. When a district expects that the adoption of a standards-based program will improve student test scores, the assumption is that the program is being implemented fully—i.e., that it is being used in the classroom in a way that is consistent with the developers' intentions. It is unreasonable to expect increases in student test scores if teachers are using the new materials infrequently (in some districts, teachers quietly put the new programs back on the shelf and returned to their familiar textbooks). It is also unreasonable to expect increases in the first year or two of implementation when pacing issues may leave teachers unable to complete the whole year's work and when teachers also have to contend with unfamiliar ways of working with their class. Collecting data about how implementation is progressing will help you adjust your expectations for student performance during the first few years of the process.

By checking in regularly with teachers, you will stay abreast of the particular implementation challenges they are facing and can plan ways to support them as they grapple with these challenges. Several ways to do this are outlined below.

Grade-Level Curriculum Meetings

Many districts have found grade-level meetings to be an important forum for discussing implementation issues. Teachers can use these meetings to check in with each other about how their classroom implementation is going, talk about pacing and management issues, discuss problems or questions, and share strategies for making the program run smoothly and effectively. All of this information is useful for monitoring the implementation process, so make sure you get feedback and input from every teacher involved in the implementation.

It is important to have written documentation so that you can remember when and where certain issues arose, follow their evolution over time, and note the strategies and solutions that teachers develop. Written notes of meetings can serve as your data; we recommend that someone take specific responsibility for attending meetings with the intention of documenting implementation issues, questions, and strategies.

Classroom Observations

By visiting mathematics classes, you can see how teachers are transforming the paper curriculum into actual classroom work and how students are responding to lessons that provide opportunities for investigation and problem solving, collaborative work, and mathematical discussion. There are several aspects of classroom activity to which you should pay particular attention:

- **Organization and rhythm of the classroom:** How smoothly did the teacher set up and manage the lesson? Are needed materials available and accessible? Is the room organized to facilitate students' work? Do students know where they are supposed to go and what they are supposed to do?

- **Mathematical motivation for the lesson:** Does the teacher have a clear sense of the mathematical purpose of the lesson? Does the teacher focus on the central mathematical ideas when interacting with students?

- **Students' mathematical work:** Do you find evidence of students' mathematical thinking in their written work and in their conversations with the teacher, their classmates, and classroom visitors?

- **Attitudes and work habits:** Are students engaged in the lesson and working hard?

> *I have audiotaped children doing wonderful things. They'll come up to the recorder with no notes and say, "This is what I did and this is how I did it and this is what I got." It's the students' ownership that's cool. (A.S., district mathematics supervisor)*

Interviews and Informal Conversations with Teachers and Students

After you visit a teacher's classroom, debrief about the lesson. Point out aspects of the lesson that were interesting and thought-provoking. Conversations with teachers about their practice can often provide insights into the pedagogical and content issues they are grappling with. In the context of your conversation about the lesson, find out whether there are specific issues or areas with which the teacher would like help.

A word of caution: Observations and debriefings can be very stressful for teachers, particularly if they feel they are being evaluated rather than assisted. You must strive to frame your discussion in terms of mutual interest and inquiry if you hope to have teachers openly share their concerns (see also, "Ongoing Implementation" in Chapter 9, "Teacher Support").

Questionnaires and Written Surveys

Like face-to-face interviews, questionnaires or other short, written descriptions of implementation experiences can offer a standardized format for teachers to share their thoughts and feelings. They also have the advantage of being less time-intensive than conducting individual observations or interviews. The disadvantage is that answers may be short or difficult to interpret. Also, questionnaires are only useful when people take the time to complete and return them. The more you can arrange to make it easy for people to get their responses to you, the more information you will have about implementation.

Use questionnaires to keep track of details of classroom implementation: how long it is taking teachers to complete particular units; what specific questions or issues arise with different units; which aspects of the curriculum are working well for teachers and which are problematic; and what teachers really like about the curriculum and what they do not. Also, ask teachers for suggestions about how to make the implementation more effective.

Remember that the way you frame your questions can affect the kinds of responses you'll get. You'll get more detailed information if you word your questions to avoid "yes" and "no" responses (for example, instead of asking, "Are you experiencing any challenges in using this curriculum?" you can ask "What challenges are you experiencing?"). Questionnaires are a particularly good source of information if you are looking for an overall impression of how implementation is proceeding. If you want more detailed information about certain issues, talk with teachers individually or raise your questions in staff meetings.

Collecting Information from Parents

Parents offer another source of information about program implementation. Look for changes in the amount of expressed support for the program and in the types (and quantity) of concerns that parents express. One district monitored parents' calls to the high school requesting that their children be placed in traditional mathematics classes, despite teachers' recommendations that the students enroll in the standards-based program. The largest number of requests occurred in the first year of the program and the number of requests diminished steadily afterward. By the fourth year of implementation, word had spread around the district that the students in standards-based courses were indeed learning mathematics, scoring well on tests, and gaining college admission, and there were no requests to shift students' course assignments. You can collect information from parents in a number of ways:

- Keep logs of visits, letters, and phone calls to principals, department chairs, and central office administrators. When parents have questions or concerns, keep track of the kinds of issues they are raising and note any changes over time. Also note parents' expressions of interest and support for the program.

- Check with teachers about their conversations with parents: What are parents' concerns, how pressing do these concerns feel, and what kinds of support for the program are parents expressing?

- Send short questionnaires to parents to ask about their children's mathematical education.

Planning Your Data Collection

If designing and carrying out data collection is new to you, it may seem like a tall order. In fact, much of the process relies on common sense and your own experience and judgment. The biggest challenge may lie in taking a more systematic approach to the questions you are asking and in focusing particularly on changes in teaching and learning as the implementation proceeds. You will be asking many of the same questions you have always asked about adopting a new curriculum—what are teachers' reactions to the materials, how well are students mastering the mathematics, and are parents satisfied with their children's learning? Taking a standards-based approach to mathematics education may lead you to articulate your goals and expectations in somewhat new ways, which, in turn, will lead you to look for new or different kinds of information to answer these familiar questions. For example, you will not only want to know how well students can solve standard problems but also how well they can reason, describe, and discuss their mathematical ideas; whether they are engaged and confident mathematicians; and how able they are to work collaboratively as well as individually on mathematical investigations and nonstandard problem-solving situations.

If you need some help deciding what kinds of data to collect and how to collect it, various people and organizations can help you get started:

- **The research and evaluation department in your school district.** Some districts, particularly larger ones, have an internal research and evaluation department that is responsible for evaluating school programs. If your district has such a department, it may even be charged with taking the lead on collecting information about implementation of new mathematics programs. Consult with evaluators about the kind(s) of information you will find most useful.

- **Expert community members.** Parents or businesspeople within your community may have the necessary skills and knowledge to help you collect data about implementation. Calling on their expertise not only helps your implementation process but provides a way to increase community involvement.

- **Colleagues in other school systems.** Talk with colleagues in other districts about the kinds of information they are collecting and the data collection strategies they are using. Consulting with others can help you sharpen your own ideas about the information you will find most useful.

- **University partners.** If you have access to university faculty or educational specialists from nearby research and development organizations, consult with them about how to shape your data collection. Graduate students may even be eager to participate in a research effort at little or no cost to the district.

Afterword

Unless you're one of those people whose first impulse on getting a new book is to flip to the back to find out how it ends, by the time you read this you will have encountered many pages' worth of observations and suggestions about selecting and implementing new mathematics materials. We trust that you recognize that adopting a standards-based curriculum is both worthwhile and challenging, and we hope that you will feel supported and encouraged to pursue the adoption of standards-based materials in your district or school.

In these pages, we have tried to offer you some insight into how differences in the content, pedagogical approach, and organization of standards-based mathematics curricula can affect your adoption process, and to provide some images of how other districts have negotiated aspects of their own adoption processes. We hope that we have also been able to provide you with some guiding principles for organizing your selection and implementation.

It is important to recognize that, while having high quality curriculum materials can go a long way toward improving mathematics education in your district, the materials will not carry the effort on their own. The new curriculum is not a silver bullet. Without quality teaching, assessment practices that are consistent with the content and pedagogy of the curriculum, district policies and practices that support teachers and students, and community support, your curriculum will be no more than words on the page and some accompanying bits of plastic, wood, and circuitry. Keep in mind that your curriculum is simply a tool to help you achieve your district's goal of improving mathematics learning for your students.

As we have worked with districts throughout the country, we have observed a sense of camaraderie and connection among people who are engaged in bringing mathematics reform to classrooms in their districts. We hope that, on finishing this guide, you have the sense that there are a variety of resources available to support you. There are an increasing number of print materials, videotapes, and websites dedicated to promoting mathematics education reform. In addition, educators who see the move toward mathematics education reform as a means for improving students' mathematical literacy and increasing interest and engagement in mathematics are generally quite eager to share with others their experiences and the lessons they have learned from their efforts to make standards-based mathematics curricula work in their districts. Take advantage of these resources, and seek out the advice and assistance of colleagues in districts that are already using standards-based programs. Soon you will be able to return the favor for others!

Acknowledgments

Our preparation of this guide has benefitted enormously from the expertise, advice, and thoughtful critiques of a number of colleagues. As a product of the K–12 Mathematics Curriculum Center, it represents the collective ideas and efforts of the Center staff: Deborah Bryant, Pamela Frorer, Grace Kelemanik, Richard King, Shirley Lee, Ki McClennan, Rebecca Moss, and Kristin Winkler; and Nancy Belkov and Barbara Miller, who comprise our evaluation team. It has been a pleasure to be part of this group and to have had the opportunity to learn from, and with, them all.

We have had the assistance of colleagues who have admirably discharged their responsibilities as "critical friends," carefully reading earlier drafts of this guide and commenting on its contents from different perspectives, some from positions inside school districts and others as outside supporters of districts' efforts to embrace mathematics education reform. Margaret (Peg) Bondorew, Mark Driscoll, Joanne Gurry, Joan Miller, Terry Nowak, Leah Quinn, Faye Ruopp, and Albert Taborn all freely shared their experiences and their thoughts, offered helpful advice, and gave generously of their time. Additional thanks go to Gerald Kulm from Project 2061 and Charles Rooney from FairTest. Thank you also to John (Spud) Bradley, program officer at the National Science Foundation, for his ongoing support of our work.

Kristin Winkler has ably shepherded this guide through every stage of production. Jennifer Davis-Kay has exercised her red pen with respectful diligence, and Andrea Parker is the fastest "copy editing enterer" ever. Thanks are owed also to Sara Kennedy for her assistance with research and permissions.

Finally, we would like to thank all of the teachers, mathematics supervisors, associate superintendents for curriculum and instruction, principals, and district consultants who have helped us to understand their experiences in selecting and implementing standards-based curricula. Their efforts, at the leading edge of mathematics education reform, have made this guide possible.

Lynn Goldsmith

June Mark

Ilene Kantrov

Appendices

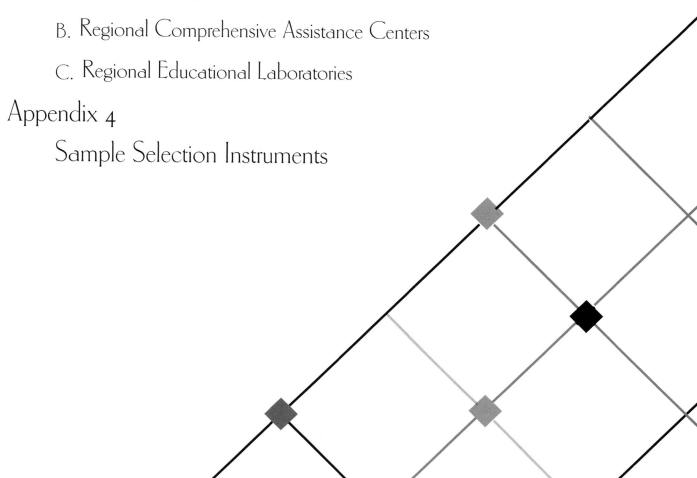

APPENDIX 1:

Implementation Centers funded by the National Science Foundation

K-12

The K-12 Mathematics Curriculum Center (K-12 MCC)

Contact: Ki McClennan
K–12 Mathematics Curriculum Center
Education Development Center, Inc.
55 Chapel Street
Newton, MA 02458-1060
phone: (800) 332-2429
fax: (617) 969-1527
email: mcc@edc.org
URL: http://www.edc.org/mcc

Established in 1997 by Education Development Center, Inc., the K–12 Mathematics Curriculum Center supports school districts as they build effective mathematics education programs using curricula that respond to and align with the National Council of Teachers of Mathematics' Curriculum and Evaluation Standards for School Mathematics. For more information about our products and services, please see the cover page of this publication.

Elementary

The ARC Center (Alternatives for Rebuilding Curricula)

Contact: Sheila Sconiers
COMAP, Inc.
57 Bedford Street, Suite 210
Lexington, MA 02420
phone: (800) 772-6627, ext. 50
fax: (781) 863-1202
e-mail: arccenter@mail.comap.com
URL: http://www.arccenter.comap.com

The ARC Center is a collaboration between the Consortium for Mathematics and its Applications (COMAP) and the three NSF-supported elementary mathematics curriculum projects, Everyday Mathematics (University of Chicago); Investigations in Number, Data and Space (TERC); and Math Trailblazers (University of Illinois at Chicago). The collaboration aims to promote the wide-scale implementation of reform elementary mathematics curricula.

(continued)

Middle

Show-Me Center (National Center for Standards-based Middle Grades Mathematics Curricula)

Contact: Barbara Reys
University of Missouri
104 Stewart Hall
Columbia, MO 65211
phone: (573) 884-2099
fax: (573) 882-4481
e-mail: center@showme.missouri.edu
http://showmecenter.missouri.edu/

The Show-Me Center, in partnership with five NSF-sponsored middle grades curriculum development satellites (University of Wisconsin, Michigan State University, University of Montana, Institute for Research on Learning, Education Development Center) and their publishers provides information and resources needed to support selection and implementation of standards-based middle grades mathematics curricula.

High

COMPASS (Curricular Options in Mathematics Programs for All Secondary Students)

Contact: Eric Robinson
Ithaca College
306 Williams Hall
Ithaca, NY 14850-7284
phone: (800) 688-1829; (607) 274-1513
fax: (607) 274-3054
e-mail: compass@ithaca.edu
http://www.ithaca.edu/compass

COMPASS is a secondary school implementation project funded in part by the National Science Foundation. The COMPASS implementation project partners with a satellite site for each of the five secondary-level curricula. The primary function of the COMPASS project is to inform schools, districts, teachers, parents, administrators, state offices, and other groups about these innovative curricula; aid in the first general phases of implementation; and coordinate requests for additional information and assistance from the satellite sites.

New England Region
IMPACT

Claire Duggan, Project Director
716 Columbus Avenue #378
Boston, MA 02120
phone: (617) 373-2036
fax: (617) 373-8496
email: cduggan@lynx.neu.edu
http://www.neu.edu/cesame
http://test-projects.terc.edu/impact

The five year IMPACT project seeks to create a sustainable, widespread implementation capacity resulting in over 250,000 students in New England using standards-based instructional materials. The Center for the Enhancement of Science and Mathematics Education (CESAME) will use its experience in the selection and implementation of standards-based curricula to develop and support this scaled-up regional effort. IMPACT's design builds on existing regional structures to provide the information, resources and support for districts and their teachers in this next step in reform.

Appendix 2

Curriculum-specific Satellite Implementation Centers Funded by the National Science Foundation

Elementary School Level

Everyday Mathematics

Andy Isaacs
University of Chicago School Mathematics Project
5835 South Kimbark Avenue
Chicago, IL 60637
phone: (773) 702-9639
fax: (773) 702-4312
e-mail: aisaacs@uchicago.edu

Investigations in Number, Data and Space

Lorraine Brooks
Administrative Assistant
TERC
2067 Massachusetts Avenue
Cambridge, MA 02140
phone: (617) 547-0430
fax: (617) 349-3535
e-mail: lorraine_brooks@terc.edu

Math Trailblazers

Joan Bieler
Co-Director
Teaching Integrated Mathematics and Science Project
Institute for Mathematics and Science Education
University of Illinois at Chicago
950 South Halsted, Rm. 2075 SEL m/c 250
Chicago, IL 60607
phone: (312) 413-2970
fax: (312) 413-7411
e-mail: jbieler@uic.edu

Middle School Level

Connected Mathematics

Elizabeth Phillips
Senior Academic Specialist
Connected Mathematics Project
Michigan State University
Mathematics Department, A715 Wells Hall
East Lansing, MI 48824-1050
phone: (517) 353-3835
fax: (517) 432-2872
e-mail: ephillip@math.msu.edu

Mathematics in Context

Meg Meyer
MiC Project Coordinator
Mathematics in Context Satellite Center
Wisconsin Center for Education Research
1025 West Johnson Street
Madison, WI 53706
phone: (608) 263-1798
fax: (608) 263-3406
e-mail: mrmeyer@macc.wisc.edu

MathScape: Seeing and Thinking Mathematically

Susan Janssen
Associate Project Director
MathScape/STM Curriculum Center
Education Development Center, Inc.
55 Chapel Street
Newton, MA 02458-1060
phone: (617) 969-7100, ext. 2553
fax: (617) 965-6325
e-mail: sjanssen@edc.org

Middle School Level, cont.

MATHThematics

Rick Billstein
Director
STEM Project: Six Through Eight Mathematics
Mathematics Department
University of Montana
Missoula, MT 59812
phone: (406) 243-2603
fax: (406) 243-2674
e-mail: rickb@selway.umt.edu

Middle-school Mathematics through Applications

Jennifer Knudsen
Director, MMAP Implementation Center
The Institute for Research on Learning
66 Willow Place
Menlo Park, CA 94025
phone: (650) 687-7918
fax: (650) 687-7957
e-mail: jennifer_knudsen@irl.org

High School Level

Contemporary Mathematics in Context (Core-Plus)

Beth Ritsema
CPMP Professional Development Coordinator
Department of Mathematics and Statistics
Western Michigan University
Kalamazoo, MI 49008
phone: (616) 387-4562
fax: (616) 387-4530
e-mail: cpmp@wmich.edu

Interactive Mathematics Program (IMP)

Janice Bussey, Outreach Coordinator
Interactive Mathematics Program Satellite Center
P.O. Box 2891
Sausalito, CA 94966
phone: (888) 628-4467
fax: (415) 332-3381
e-mail: imp@math.sfsu.edu

MATH Connections: A Secondary Mathematics Core Curriculum

June Ellis, Ph.D., Principal Investigator
MATH Connections Implementation Center
Mathconx LLC
750 Old Main Street, Suite 303
Rocky Hill, CT   06067-1567
phone: (860) 721-7010
fax: (860) 721-7026
e-mail: mathconx@aol.com

Mathematics: Modeling Our World (ARISE)

Linda Vahey, Marketing Director, Special Projects
Consortium for Mathematics and Its Applications (COMAP) Inc.
57 Bedford Street, Suite 210
Lexington, MA 02173
phone: (800) 772-6627; (781) 862-7878
fax: (781) 863-1202
e-mail: info@comap.com

SIMMS Integrated Mathematics

Gary Bauer, Director
SIMMS Integrated Mathematics Dissemination
401 Linfield Hall
Montana State University-Bozeman
Bozeman, MT 59717-0281
phone: (800) 693-4060
fax: (406) 994-3733
e-mail: gbauer@math.montana.edu

APPENDIX 3

Regional Centers Funded by the U.S. Department of Education

A. Eisenhower Mathematics and Science Education Regional Consortia and Clearinghouse Programs

Northeastern Region

The Eisenhower Regional Alliance for Better School-Based Mathematics and Science Reform

Region: CT, ME, MA, NH, NY, RI, VT, PR and the VI
Mark Kaufman, Project Director
TERC
2067 Massachusetts Avenue
Cambridge, MA 02140
phone: (617) 547-0430
fax: (617) 349-3535
URL: http://ra.terc.edu

Mid-Atlantic Region

The Mid-Atlantic Eisenhower Regional Consortium for Mathematics and Science Education

Region: DE, MD, NJ, PA and DC
Keith Kirschner, Project Director
Research for Better Schools (RBS)
444 North Third Street
Philadelphia, PA 19123
phone: (215) 574-9300 x 279
fax: (215) 574-0133
URL: http://www.rbs.org/eisenhower/

Southeastern Region

Southeast Mathematics and Science Regional Consortium

Region: AL, FL, GA, MS, NC and SC
Francena Cummings, Project Director
Southeastern Regional Vision for Education (SERVE)
345 South Magnolia Drive, Suite D-23
Tallahassee, FL 32301-2950
phone: (904) 671-6033
fax: (904) 671-6010
URL: http://www.serve.org/Eisenhower/

Appalachian Region

Eisenhower Regional Consortium for Mathematics and Science

Region: KY, TN, VA and WV
Appalachia Educational Laboratory, Inc. (AEL)
Pam Buckley, Project Director
1031 Quarrier Street
Charleston, WV 25325
phone: (304) 347-0400; (800) 624-8120
fax: (304) 347-0487
URL: http://www.ael.org/eisen/

Midwestern Region

The Midwest Consortium for Mathematics and Science Education

Region: IA, IL, IN, MI, MN, WI and OH
Gil Valdez, Project Director
North Central Regional Educational Laboratory (NCREL)
1900 Spring Road, Suite 300
Oak Brook, IL 60521
phone: (708) 218-1024
fax: (708) 571-4716
URL: http://www.ncrel.org/ncrel/msc/msc.htm

Central Region

The Eisenhower Consortium for Mathematics and Science Education

Region: CO, KS, MO, NE, ND, SD and WY
John Sutton, Project Director
Mid-Continental Regional Educational Laboratory (McREL)
2550 South Parker Road, Suite 500
Aurora, CO 80014
phone: (800) 949-6387
fax: (303) 337-3005
URL: http://www.mcrel.org/hpc

Northwestern Region

Science and Mathematics Consortium for Northwest Schools (SMCNWS)

Region: AK, ID, MT, OR and WA
Ralph Nelsen, Project Director
Columbia Education Center (CEC)
11325 SE Lexington
Portland, OR 97266-5927
phone: (503) 760-2346
fax: (503) 760-5592
URL: http://www.col-ed.org/smcnws/

Western Region

Far West Eisenhower Regional Consortium for Science and Mathematics Education (FWERC)

Region: AZ, CA, NV and UT
Art Sussman, Project Director
Far West Laboratory for Educational Research and Development (FWL)
730 Harrison Street
San Francisco, CA 94107
phone: (415) 241-2728
fax: (415) 565-3012
URL: http://www.wested.org/werc/

Southwestern Region

Eisenhower Southwest Consortium for the Improvement of Mathematics and Science Teaching

Region: AR, LA, NM, OK and TX
Wes Hoover, Project Director
Southwest Educational Development Laboratory (SEDL)
211 East Seventh Street
Austin, TX 78701-3281
phone: (512) 476-6861
fax: (512) 476-2286
URL: http://www.sedl.org/pitl/scimast/welcome.html

Pacific Region

Eisenhower Regional Consortium for Mathematics and Science Education

Region: HI, American Samoa, Commonwealth of the Northern Mariana Islands, Federated States of Micronesia, Guam, Republic of the Marshall Islands and the Republic of Palau
Paul Dumas, Project Director
Pacific Region Educational Laboratory (PREL)
828 Fort Street Mall, Suite 500
Honolulu, HI 96813
phone: (808) 533-6000 x 132
fax: (808) 533-7599
URL: http://w3.prel.hawaii.edu/programs/math-science.html

B. Regional Comprehensive Assistance Centers

Region 1

Connecticut, Maine, Massachusetts, New Hampshire,
Rhode Island, Vermont
Wende Allen, Director
NECAC at EDC, Inc.
55 Chapel Street
Newton, MA 02458-1060
phone: (800) 332-0226 x2533
fax: (617) 965-6325
e-mail: WAllen@edc.org

Region 2

New York
LaMar Miller, Executive Director
Region 02 Comprehensive Center
New York University
82 Washington Square East, Suite 72
New York, NY 10003
phone: (800) 469-8224
fax: (212) 995-4199
e-mail: millrla@is2.nyu.edu

Region 3

Delaware, Maryland, New Jersey, Ohio, Pennsylvania,
Washington, D.C.
Charlene Rivera, Director
Region 03 Evaluation Assistance Center/East
George Washington University
1730 North Lynn Street, Suite 401
Arlington, VA 22209
phone: (703) 528-3588
fax: (703) 528-5973
e-mail: crivera@ceee.gwu.edu

Region 4

Kentucky, North Carolina, South Carolina, Tennessee,
Virginia, West Virginia
Pamela Buckley, Director, Eisenhower Regional
Region 04 Comprehensive Center
Appalachia Educational Laboratory
P.O. Box 1348
Charleston, WV 25325-1348
phone: (800) 624-9120
fax: (304) 347-1888
e-mail: buckleyp@ael.org

Region 5

Alabama, Arkansas, Georgia, Louisiana, Mississippi
Hai Tran, Director
Region 05 Comprehensive Center
3330 Causeway Boulevard, Suite 430
Metairie, LA 70002-3573
phone: (800) 644-8671
fax: (504) 831-5242
e-mail: htran@sedl.org

Region 6

Iowa, Michigan, Minnesota, North Dakota, South
Dakota, Wisconsin
Walter Secada, Director
Region 06 Comprehensive Center
University of Wisconsin
1025 West Johnson Street
Madison, WI 53706
phone: (608) 263-4220
fax: (608) 263-3733
e-mail: wgsecada@facstaff.wisc.edu

Region 7

Illinois, Indiana, Kansas, Missouri, Nebraska, Oklahoma
Belinda Biscoe, Director
Region 07 Comprehensive Center
University of Oklahoma
555 Constitution Street, Suite 128
Norman, OK 73077-0005
phone: (405) 325-1711
fax: (405) 325-1824
e-mail: biscoe@uoknor.edu

Region 8

Texas
Albert Cortez, Director
Region 08 Comprehensive Center
Intercultural Development Research Association
5835 Callagham Road, Suite 350
San Antonio, TX 78228-1190
phone: (210) 684-8180
fax: (210) 684-5389
e-mail: acortez@idra.org

Region 9

Arizona, Colorado, New Mexico, Nevada, Utah
Paul Martinez, Director
Region 09 Comprehensive Center
Southwest Comprehensive Center
1700 Grande Court
Rio Rancho, NM 87124
phone: (800) 247-4269
fax: (505) 891-5744
e-mail: pmartinez@cesdp.nmhu.edu

Region 10

Idaho, Montana, Oregon, Washington, Wyoming
Carlos Sundermann, Director
Region 10 Comprehensive Center
Northwest Regional Educational Lab
101 Southwest Main Street, Suite 500
Portland, OR 97204
phone: (503) 275-9587
fax: (503) 275-9625
e-mail: sundermc@nwrel.org

Region 11

Northern California
Beverly Cole, Director
Region 11 Comprehensive Center
Far West Lab for Educational Research
730 Harrison Street
San Francisco, CA 94107-1242
phone: (800) 64L-EARN
fax: (415) 565-3012
e-mail: bfarr@WestEd.org

Region 12

Southern California
Henry Mothner, Director
Region 12 Comprehensive Center
Los Angeles County Office of Education
9300 Imperial Highway, EC 299
Downey, CA 90242-2890
phone: (562) 922-6343
fax: (562) 940-1798
e-mail: mothner_henry@lacoe.edu

Region 13

Alaska
JoAnn Henderson, Director
Region 13 Comprehensive Center
210 Ferry Way, Suite 200
Juneau, AK 99801
phone: (907) 586-6806
fax: (907) 463-3811
e-mail: joannh@akrac.k12.ak.us

Region 14

Florida, Puerto Rico, Virgin Islands
Trudy Hensley, Director
Region 14 Comprehensive Center
Educational Testing Service
1979 Lake Side Parkway, Suite 400
Tucker, GA 30084
phone: (800) 241-3865
fax: (770) 723-7436
e-mail: thensley@ets.org

Region 15

American Samoa, Federated States of Micronesia, Commonwealth of the Northern Mariana Islands, Guam, Hawaii, Republic of the Marshall Islands, Republic of Palau
Tom Barlow, Director
Region 15 Comprehensive Center
Eastern Pacific Service Center
828 Fort Street Mall, Suite 500
Honolulu, HI 96813-4321
phone: (808) 533-6000
fax: (808) 533-7599
e-mail: barlowt@prel.hawaii.edu

C. Regional Educational Laboratories

Appalachian Region

Appalachia Educational Laboratory, Inc. (AEL)

Executive Director: Dr. Terry Eidell
1031 Quarrier Street
P.O. Box 1348
Charleston, WV 25325
phone: (304) 347-0400 or (800) 624-9120
fax: (304) 347-0487
States Served: KY, TN, VA, WV
Specialty Area: Rural Education

Western Region

WestEd

Executive Director: Dr. Glen H. Harvey E.D.
Inquiries: Tom Ross
730 Harrison Street
San Francisco, CA 94107
phone: (415) 565-3000
fax: (415) 565-3012
States Served: AZ, CA, NV, UT
Specialty Area: Assessment and Accountability

Central Region

Mid-continent Regional Educational Laboratory (McREL)

Executive Director: Dr. J. Timothy Waters
2550 South Parker Road, Suite 500
Aurora, CO 80014
phone: (303) 337-0990
fax: (303) 337-3005
States Served: CO, KS, MO, NE, ND, SD, WY
Specialty Area: Curriculum, Learning and Instruction

Midwestern Region

North Central Regional Educational Laboratory (NCREL)

Dr. Jeri Nowakowski
1900 Spring Road, Suite 300
Oak Brook, IL 60521
phone: (630) 571-4700
fax: (630) 571-4716
States Served: IA, IL, IN, MI, MN, OH, WI
Specialty Area: Technology

Northwestern Region

Northwest Regional Educational Laboratory (NWREL)

Executive Director: Dr. Ethel Simon-McWilliams
101 SW Main Street, Suite 500
Portland, OR 97204
phone: (503) 275-9500; (800) 547-6339
fax: (503) 275-9489
States Served: AK, ID, MT, OR, WA
Specialty Area: School Change Processes

Pacific Region

Pacific Resources for Education & Learning (PREL)

Executive Director: Dr. John Kofel
1099 Alakea Street, Suite 2500
Honolulu, HI 96813
phone: (808) 533-6000
fax: (808) 533-7599
States Served: American Samoa, Commonwealth of the Northern Mariana Islands, Federated States of Micronesia, Guam, Hawaii, Republic of the Marshall Islands, Republic of Palau
Specialty Area: Language and Cultural Diversity

Northeastern Region

Lab at Brown University Education Alliance (LAB)

Executive Director: Dr. Phil Zarlengo
222 Richmond Street, Suite 300
Providence, RI 02903
phone: (401) 274-9548 or (800) 521-9550
fax: (401) 421-7650
States Served: CT, MA, ME, NH, NY, PR, RI, VI, VT
Specialty Area: Language and Cultural Diversity

Mid-Atlantic Region

The Laboratory for Student Success (LSS)

Executive Director: Dr. Margaret Wang
933 Ritter Annex, 13th and Cecil B. Moore
Philadelphia, PA 19122
phone: (215) 204-3001
States Served: DC, DE, MD, NJ, PA
Specialty Area: Urban Education

Southeastern Region

SouthEastern Regional Vision for Education (SERVE)

Executive Director: Don Holznagel, Interim Director
P.O. Box 5367
Greensboro, NC 27435
phone: (910) 334-3211; (800) 755-3277
fax: (910) 334-3268
States Served: AL, FL, GA, MS, NC, SC
Specialty Area: Early Childhood Education

Southwestern Region

Southwest Educational Development Laboratory (SEDL)

Executive Director: Dr. Wesley A. Hoover
211 East Seventh Street
Austin, TX 78701
phone: (512) 476-6861
fax: (512) 476-2286
States Served: AR, LA, NM, OK, TX
Specialty Area: Language and Cultural Diversity

Appendix 4

Sample Selection Instruments

Elementary Program Selection Criteria

reprinted with permission from Arlington Public Schools, Arlington, MA

K-8 Mathematics Adoption Pilot Evaluation

reprinted with permission from San Diego City Schools, San Diego, CA

Mathematics Materials Selection Criteria

reprinted with permission from Missoula County Public Schools, Missoula, MT

Reaching Every Teacher High School Selection Criteria

reprinted with permission from Waltham Public Schools, Waltham, MA, and Education Development Center, Inc., Newton, MA

Project 2061 Curriculum Selection Criteria

reprinted with permission from the American Association for the Advancement of Science

Evaluation Criteria from the U.S. Department of Education's Expert Panel on Mathematics and Science Education

in the public domain

Text:_____ Name:_____

SMALL GROUP ISSUES   Date:_____

NUMBER SENSE & NUMERATION	PATTERNS & RELATIONSHIPS
1. How does the program develop understanding of the <u>numeration system (counting, grouping, regrouping, place value)</u>?	1. To what extent does the program use <u>patterns, variables, open sentences, number sentences, and relationships</u> to explore mathematics?
2. How does the program develop understanding of the <u>numeration system</u>? (+, -, x, ÷)	2. How does the program use <u>tables, graphs, rules, and equations</u> to represent situations and to <u>solve and model problems</u>?
3. How does the program develop understanding of: fractions, mixed numbers, decimals, percents, integers, and rational numbers?	3. How does the program develop understanding of the <u>solving of linear equations</u>, using concrete, informal and formal methods?

NUMBER SENSE & NUMERATION (cont.)	
4. How does the program model, explain and develop understanding of <u>basic facts & algorithms</u>?	
5. How does the program build understanding of the <u>representation of numerical relationships on graphs</u>?	
6. How does the program give practice in selection and use of appropriate <u>methods for computing</u>: mental arithmetic paper & pencil manipulative calculator computer other	
7. How does the program teach <u>estimation</u> to check the reasonableness of results?	

GEOMETRY & MEASUREMENT	STATISTICS & PROBABILITY
1. How does the program develop understanding of how to <u>describe, model, compare and classify</u> shapes?	1. How does the program provide experiences in collecting, organizing, describing, and interpreting displays of data?
2. How does the program use the process of measuring and concepts related to units of <u>measurement</u>?	2. How does the program teach students to make inferences and construct arguments based on <u>data analysis</u>?
3. How does the program demonstrate understanding of <u>perimeter, area, volume, angle</u>?	

Text: _____   NAME _____

_____   DATE _____

GENERAL LEARNING ISSUES

1. To what extent does program set <u>high expectations</u> for students?	
2. How does the program help students to learn through a <u>variety of strategies and approaches</u>?	
3. a. To what extent does the program foster learning that is based on <u>inquiry</u>?	
b. <u>Problem-solving</u>?	
c. <u>Application of key issues and concepts</u>?	
4. How does the program point to <u>connections</u> between math topics & across the disciplines to other subjects?	
5. How does this program support <u>all learners</u> at <u>all levels</u>?	
6. a. How does this program broaden understanding of mathematics in a <u>cultural context</u>?	
b. Our culture?	
c. Other cultures?	
7. In which ways does the program foster mathematical thinking through technology (calculators & computers)?	
8. a. To what extent is student <u>mathematical discussion and interaction</u> fostered in the classroom?	
b. Is discussion <u>essential</u> to learning <u>or</u> is it an <u>added</u> activity?	
9. What kinds of <u>teacher mathematical communication and student-teacher interaction</u> [are] fostered in the classroom?	
10. To what extent is writing about math fostered?	

IMPLEMENTATION

1. How does this program assist the teacher to <u>understand and manage</u> all of its components?	
2. What <u>information</u> is <u>sent home</u> to parents about children's learning?	
3. a. How does the program foster students' application of mathematics learning at home? b. On their Own? c. With their parents?	
4. What <u>transitions from current practice</u> will our staff need to make to teach this program?	
5. What kinds of in-service plan would this program require to insure successful implementation?	
6. a. How should the program be introduced? b. Which grades? c. In which order?	
7. What communication to parents is available to explain this program?	

ASSESSMENT

1. a. What assessment <u>practices</u> are used?	
b. Are they <u>consistent</u> with instructional practices?	
2. To what extent does the program help students to <u>understand</u> <u>for themselves</u> what they know and don't know?	
3. To what extent does the program offer a <u>comprehensive</u> <u>approach</u> to assessment? (i.e., providing any perspectives to understand students' progress?)	

reprinted with permission from Arlington Public Schools, Arlington, MA

SUMMARY

1. What is the overall program structure for the understanding of mathematics, e.g.
    a. linear (self-contained lesson after lesson),

_____

    b. widening spiral of topics,

_____

    c. in-depth exploration of topics over time,

_____

    d. themes or "big questions",

_____

    e. other

2. To what extent does this program offer a <u>complete or comprehensive</u> mathematics education for our students?

3. To what extent does this program prepare K-6 students for mathematics in grades 7 - 12?

4. How would our students' mathematics education be different as a consequence of adopting this program?

K-8 Mathematics Adoption Pilot Evaluation

Evaluation Prompts	Publisher:	Publisher:
1. Understanding of written materials by the students	Low 1 2 3 High 4 Comments:	Low 1 2 3 High 4 Comments:
2. Teacher friendliness of program: • directions are clear, easy to understand throughout lessons • teacher's guide is well organized, easy to use • information regarding manipulatives is accessible and sufficient • information regarding support/ supplementary materials is accessible and sufficient	Low 1 2 3 High 4 Comments:	Low 1 2 3 High 4 Comments:
3. Friendliness of student materials: • visually appealing, easy to understand • provides good directions for students • language made accessible to all students • readability is developmentally appropriate	Low 1 2 3 High 4 Comments:	Low 1 2 3 High 4 Comments:
Please answer if appropriate to your class population. 4a. Does it meet the needs of Bilingual students? 4b. Does it meet the needs of LEP students? 4c. Does it meet the needs of Spec. Ed. students? 4d. Does it meet the needs of GATE students?	4a. Low 1 2 3 High 4 4b. Low 1 2 3 High 4 4c. Low 1 2 3 High 4 4d. Low 1 2 3 High 4 Comments:	4a. Low 1 2 3 High 4 4b. Low 1 2 3 High 4 4c. Low 1 2 3 High 4 4d. Low 1 2 3 High 4 Comments:

reprinted with permission from San Diego City Schools, San Diego, CA

Evaluation Prompts	Publisher:	Publisher:
5a. Use of manipulatives as provided by program.	5a. Difficult 1　2　3　4 Easy	5a. Difficult 1　2　3　4 Easy
5b. Availability of manipulatives not supplied by the program.	5b. Inaccessible 1　2　3　4 Accessible	5b. Inaccessible 1　2　3　4 Accessible
5c. Amount of time spent duplicating materials that are essential to the program.	5c. Above Average 1　2　3　4 Below Average　Comments:	5c. Above Average 1　2　3　4 Below Average　Comments:
6. Adequacy of support materials: • materials other than the teacher's edition & kit materials, i.e., videotapes, audio tapes, trade books, etc.	Low 1　2　3　4 High　Comments:	Low 1　2　3　4 High　Comments:
7. A variety of assessment techniques are included: • pre/post • embedded • performance-based • portfolios • journals • student self-evaluation, etc.	Low 1　2　3　4 High　Comments:	Low 1　2　3　4 High　Comments:
8. The teacher materials provide strategies for teacher management: • ease of preparation for setting up lessons • use of problem solving skills in activities • cooperative grouping ideas • appropriate questioning strategies • assessment management • useof technology • communication with parents, administrators	Low 1　2　3　4 High　Comments:	Low 1　2　3　4 High　Comments:
9. Overall rating of this program.	Low 1　2　3　4 High　Comments:	Low 1　2　3　4 High　Comments:

MATHEMATICS MATERIALS SELECTION CRITERIA

October 1997

DIRECTIONS: Circle one number on each scale below. The higher the number, the better that text appears to meet the philosophy and Standards and Benchmarks outlined in Missoula County Public School (MCPS) new Mathematics curriculum.

Rating Scale: 5 = high
1 = low

Category 1:   Mathematical Content

The mathematical content of the program reflects the curriculum Standards.

- **Mathematics as problem solving is built into the program at all levels.** The mathematics is developed from problem situations. Situations are sufficiently simple to be manageable but sufficiently complex to provide for diversity in approach. They are amenable to individual, small-group, or large group instruction; involve a variety of mathematical domains; and are open and flexible as to the methods to be used.

  1 2 3 4 5

- **Mathematics as communication is built into the program at all levels.** Students have many opportunities to use language to communicate their mathematical ideas. The program asks students to explain, conjecture, and defend their ideas orally and in writing. As students mature and develop, the program expects students' mathematical communication to become more formal and symbolic. Students are asked to form multiple representations of ideas, express relationships within and among representation systems, and formulate generalizations.

  1 2 3 4 5

- **Mathematics as reasoning is built into the program at all levels.** Throughout the program, students are asked to explain and justify their thinking and to question the statements of other students and the teacher. As students mature, the program asks students to do both inductive and deductive reasoning. In Grades 9-12, the program expects mathematically mature students to use informal and formal arguments to support conclusions.

  1 2 3 4 5

- **Mathematical connections are clear in the program;** the program approaches mathematics as a whole. Concepts, procedures, and intellectual processes are interrelated through specific instructional activities designed to connect ideas and procedures among different mathematical topics, with other content areas, and to life situations.

  1 2 3 4 5

- **The program is comprehensive and includes the mathematics content emphasized in the Standards at each level.**

  K-8 -- see Standards and Benchmarks
  High School -- Math I, II, and III see Standards and Benchmarks
  High School -- Advanced Math classes see Standards and Benchmarks for each class
  High School -- Topics I and Topics II classes see Standards and Benchmarks

  1 2 3 4 5

Category 2:   Organization and Structure

The program is organized into cohesive units, multi-day lessons, and worthwhile tasks.

- **The program is organized into units, modules, or other structure so that students have sufficient time to explore and investigate in-depth major mathematical ideas.** The units or modules include lessons, activities, and projects that are multi-days, emphasize that connections between mathematical concepts, and promote the attainment of several, rather than just one, instructional objectives.

  1 2 3 4 5

- **The program asks students to work on worthwhile mathematical tasks.** The tasks do not separate mathematical thinking from mathematical concepts or skills; they capture students' curiosity and invite them to speculate and to pursue their hunches. Many tasks have more than one reasonable solution. The tasks require that students reason about different strategies and outcomes, weigh the pros and cons of alternatives, and pursue particular paths.

  1 2 3 4 5

- **The instructional materials incorporate calculators and computers and other technology into the program as tools for students to use to do mathematics.** The program is designed with the expectation that calculators are available to all students at all times and that all students have access to a computer for individual and group work.

  1 2 3 4 5

- **The program is appropriate for *all* students.** All students are expected to encounter typical problem situations related to important mathematical topics. All students are expected to experience mathematics in the context of the broad, rich curriculum described in the K-8 Standards. However, the program recognizes that students will differ in the vocabulary or notations used, the complexity of their arguments, and so forth. For grades 9-12, all students participate in the core program, with explicit differentiation in terms of depth and breadth of treatment and the nature of applications for mathematically mature students.

  1 2 3 4 5

Category 3:   Student Experiences

The program emphasizes students doing rather than memorizing mathematics. Students are actively involved with mathematics.

- **The program is designed so that students are active learners.** Students are encouraged to explore and investigate mathematical ideas. They are expected to read, write, and discuss mathematics. the program asks students to conjecture, test, and build arguments about a conjecture's validity. Students are asked to reason about different strategies and outcomes, weigh the pros and cons of alternatives, and pursue varied paths when working on tasks. Students are expected to work on group and individual projects and assignments.

  1 2 3 4 5

- **Students are expected to construct their own understanding of mathematics.** The program recognizes that students approach a new task with prior knowledge and encourages students to use natural language and informal procedures.

  1 2 3 4 5

- **The program asks students to engage in mathematical discourse.** The materials ask students to talks with one another, as well as respond to the teacher. Students are expected to make public conjectures and reason with others about mathematics. Students are asked to clarify and justify their ideas orally and in writing.

  1 2 3 4 5

- **Students use manipulatives and technology to explore mathematical ideas, model mathematical situations, analyze data, calculate numerical results, and solve problems.**   Generally, students decide what tools are needed and when to use them.

  1 2 3 4 5

- **Students are expected to determine when they need to calculate in a problem and whether they require an exact or approximate answer.** Students are expected to choose an appropriate procedure when calculating, whether it is using paper-and-pencil, mental calculation, or a calculator.

  1 2 3 4 5

- **Students are expected to reflect on, make judgments about, and report on their own behavior, performance, and feelings**. Students are asked to do self-assessment on selected aspects of their experiences as one method for evaluating students performance and disposition.

  1 2 3 4 5

- **Student materials are "user friendly."** The program is at the appropriate level for students to read. Textual materials are generally well organized and attractive for students.

  1 2 3 4 5

Category 4:   **Teacher's Role**

The instructional materials provide suggestions to teachers to assist them in shifting toward the vision of teaching presented by the Standards.

● **The instructional materials provide suggestions to teachers** so that in tasks and lessons teachers can help students to:

— work together to make sense of mathematics
— rely more on themselves to determine whether something is mathematically correct
— reason mathematically
— learn to conjecture, invent, and solve problems
— connect mathematics, its ideas, and its applications to other topics within mathematics and to other disciplines

1 2 3 4 5

● **The instructional materials provide suggestions for teachers in initiating and orchestrating mathematical discourse.** The materials suggest questions that elicit, engage, and challenge students' thinking. Teachers are encouraged to regularly follow students' statements with, "Why?" and "What if?" Also, teachers should ask students to explain their thinking and reasoning.

1 2 3 4 5

● **The instructional materials provide assistance to teachers to facilitate learning by all students.** Suggestions are provided on how to use a variety of methods so that all students can contribute to the thinking of the class. Students are expected to express themselves in writing and pictorially, concretely and representationally, as well as orally. The program encourages teachers to accept and respect the thinking of all students by providing examples of how to probe students' thinking and encourage students to follow and understand each others' approaches and ideas.

1 2 3 4 5

● **The instructional materials provide suggestions to teachers for establishing a classroom learning environment focused on sense making.** Teachers are provided suggestions on how to:

— structure the time so students can grapple with significant mathematical ideas and problems
— use physical space and material in ways that facilitates students' learning
— assist students to work together collaboratively, as well as independently.

1 2 3 4 5

● **The instructional materials provide suggestions to teachers to help them reflect on what happens in the classroom so that they can adjust or adapt their teaching plans.** Teachers are provided suggestions on how to observe, listen to, and gather other information so they can assess and monitor student learning. Teachers also are provided suggestions on how to examine the effect of the task, discourse, and learning environment in promoting students' understanding of mathematics.

1 2 3 4 5

- **The instructional materials provide suggestions for how parents can be involved and kept informed about the program.**

  1 2 3 4 5

- **Teacher's guides are "user friendly."** The program is easy for the teacher to follow and offers appropriate guidance in the use and integration of various student materials and technology.

  1 2 3 4 5

Category 5: Assessment

The student assessment in the instructional materials provides teachers with information about what their students know and how they think about mathematics.

- **Student assessment is integrated into the instructional program.** Assessment activities are similar to learning activities. Assessment activities examine the extent to which students have integrated and made sense of information, whether they can apply it to situations that require reasoning and creative thinking, and whether they can use mathematics to communicate their ideas.

  1 2 3 4 5

- **Multiple means of assessment are used, informal as well as formal.** Suggestions are provided for assessing students, individually or in small groups, through observations, oral, and written work, student demonstrations of presentations, and students self-assessment. The use of calculators, computer, and manipulatives are built into assessment activities. Assessment is built into the instructional materials as a continuous, dynamic, and often informal process.

  1 2 3 4 5

- **All aspects of mathematical knowledge and how they are interrelated are assessed in the instructional materials.** However, assessment is not of separate or isolated competencies, although one aspect of mathematical knowledge might be emphasized more than another in a particular assessment. Conceptual understandings and procedural knowledge are frequently assessed through tasks that ask students to apply information about a given concept in novel situations.

  1 2 3 4 5

TOTAL POINTS EARNED FOR THIS TEXT _____/130

OVERALL RATING

** Considering the philosophy, goals, and objectives of MCPS's new Mathematics curriculum, what overall rating would you give this text?

1 2 3 4 5   6 7 8 9 10

Not appropriate for MCPS   Most appropriate for MCPS

Pros to remember for later discussion:

Cons to remember for later discussion:

reprinted with permission from Missoula County Public Schools, Missoula, MT

Name of Rater _____   School _____

The criteria by which the materials should be judged follows:

Category 1 — Mathematical Content
- Mathematics as problem solving is built into the program at all levels.
- Mathematics as communication is built into the program at all levels.
- Mathematics as reasoning is built into the program at all levels.
- Mathematical connections are clear in the program.
- The program is comprehensive and includes the mathematics content emphasized in the Standards at each level.

Category 2 — Organization and Structure
- The program is organized into units, modules, or other structure so that students have sufficient time to explore and investigate in-depth major mathematical ideas.
- The program asks students to work on worthwhile mathematical tasks.
- The instructional materials incorporate calculators and computers and other technology into the program as tools for students to use to do mathematics.
- The program is appropriate for *all* students.

Category 3 — Student Experiences
- The program is designed so that students are active learners.
- Students are expected to construct their own understanding of mathematics.
- The program asks students to engage in mathematical discourse.
- Students use manipulatives and technology to explore mathematical ideas, model mathematical situations, analyze data, calculate numerical results, and solve problems.
- Students are expected to determine when they need to calculate in a problem and whether they require an exact or approximate answer.
- Students are expected to reflect on, make judgments about, and report on their own behavior, performance, and feelings.
- Student materials are "user friendly."

Category 4 — Teacher Support
- The instructional materials provide suggestions to teachers.
- The instructional materials provide suggestions for teachers in initiating and orchestrating mathematical discourse.
- The instructional materials provide assistance to teachers to facilitate learning by all students.
- The instructional materials provide suggestions to teachers for establishing a classroom learning environment focused on sense making.
- The instructional materials provide suggestions to teachers to help them reflect on what happens in the classroom so that they can adjust or adapt their teaching plans.
- The instructional materials provide suggestions for how parents can be involved and kept informed about the program.
- Teachers' guides are "user friendly."

Category 5 — Assessment
- Student assessment is integrated into the instructional program.
- Multiple means of assessment are used, informal as well as formal.
- All aspects of mathematical knowledge and how they are interrelated are assessed in the instructional materials.

Indicate your 1st, 2nd, or 3rd choice of math program by writing the name of the company/program. If you believe that a set of materials should NOT be considered, please indicate that in your comments.

1st Choice _____

2nd Choice _____

3rd Choice _____

Please use the back side of this sheet to express ideas that you may have about the math programs that are being considered.

Please return this form to the Curriculum Office by MONDAY, APRIL 13

MCPS Middle School Mathematics Materials
Parent/Community Response Form

Name _____   Date _____

My child(ren) attend or will attend the following MCPS middle school

I am a student and will attend the following MCPS middle school

Please check one of the following:

_____   **I support the middle school mathematics materials as presented.**

_____   **I generally support the middle school mathematics materials as presented with the stipulations described below.**

_____   **I do not support the middle school mathematics materials as presented. (Please indicate areas of concern.)**

Comments:

Please fill out one of these forms for each of the curricula at your level:

Curriculum You're Looking At : _____

1. **What grade levels is this program for? (circle) K 1 2 3 4 5 6 7 8 9 10 11 12**

Which components does this program have? (√)	Curriculum Components	On which component did you base this analysis? (√)
	Teachers' guide	
	Student book	
	Reproducible masters	
	Assessment guide	
	Other resources _____	
	Other resources _____	

What lesson did you do from this program?

2. **For each content strand listed below, check off (4) whether or not it is covered in the program. Then rank how well the materials address that content:**

1	2	3	4	5
Not well-addressed		Somewhat or satisfactorily addressed		Very well-addressed

Content	Covered?		Ranking			
Algebra	❏	1	2	3	4	5
Functions	❏	1	2	3	4	5
Geometry from a synthetic perspective	❏	1	2	3	4	5
Geometry from an Algebraic perspective	❏	1	2	3	4	5
Trigonometry	❏	1	2	3	4	5
Statistics	❏	1	2	3	4	5
Probability	❏	1	2	3	4	5
Discrete mathematics	❏	1	2	3	4	5
Conceptual underpinnings of calculus	❏	1	2	3	4	5
Mathematical structure	❏	1	2	3	4	5

3. **To what extent does the curriculum address topics in mathematical depth?**

1	2	3	4	5
Not at all		Somewhat		Quite a bit

4. **How well does the program provide ongoing opportunities for students to clarify, refine, and consolidate their ideas, and to communicate through reading, writing, and discussion?**

1	2	3	4	5
Poorly		Adequately		Excellently

5. **To what extent do the materials require students to use a variety of mathematical methods to solve nonroutine problems?**

1	2	3	4	5
Not at all		Somewhat		Quite a bit

6. **To what extent do the materials ensure active student participation in learning, creating, doing mathematics?**

1	2	3	4	5
Not at all		Somewhat		Quite a bit

7. **How well do the materials provide numerous and varied experiences that encourage students to develop trust in their own mathematical thinking?**

1	2	3	4	5
Poorly		Adequately		Excellently

8. **How well does the assessment inform the teacher of his or her students' mathematical understanding and progress?**

1	2	3	4	5
Poorly		Adequately		Excellently

9. **To what extent does the curriculum include a variety of kinds of assessments, such as performance, embedded, paper/pencil quizzes and tests, portfolios, projects, student interviews, etc.?**

1	2	3	4	5
Not at all		Somewhat		Quite a bit

10. **To what extent do the materials give students opportunities to practice what they've learned? (e.g. embedded practice in lessons, extra problems, supplemental materials)**

1	2	3	4	5
Poorly		Adequately		Excellently

11. **To what extent do the materials provide sufficient and appropriate material for home work?**

1	2	3	4	5
Not at all		Somewhat		Quite a bit

12. To what extent do the materials support teacher learning?

1	2	3	4	5
Not at all		Somewhat		Quite a bit

13. To what extent is the curriculum likely to be interesting, engaging and effective for all students, regardless of gender or ethnicity?

1	2	3	4	5
Not at all		Somewhat		Quite a bit

14. How well do the materials provide guidance to the teacher about how to present the lesson?

1	2	3	4	5
Poorly		Adequately		Excellently

15. Overall, how well are the materials usable by, realistic for, and supportive of teachers?

1	2	3	4	5
Not at all		Somewhat		Very much so

16. List 3 main strengths of this curriculum: | List 3 main weaknesses of this curriculum:

17. In your opinion, what is the overall quality of these materials relative to:

	Low				High
getting students excited about mathematics?	1	2	3	4	5
encouraging student thinking?	1	2	3	4	5
quality of mathematics content?	1	2	3	4	5
quality of pedagogy?	1	2	3	4	5
quality of classroom assessments?	1	2	3	4	5
encouraging teachers to teach differently?	1	2	3	4	5

18. To what extent are you in favor of adoption and implementation of this curriculum, based on what you know so far?

1	2	3	4	5
Not at all		Somewhat		Very much so

The Project 2061 Curriculum-Analysis Procedure

Introduction

Deciding which curriculum materials to use is one of the most important professional judgments that educators make. Textbook adoption committees make recommendations that influence instruction for years to come, and the daily decisions teachers make about which teaching units or chapters to use and how to use them largely determine what and how students will be expected to learn.

Such important decisions require a valid and reliable method for evaluating the quality of curriculum materials. Even an in-depth review of the topics covered by a textbook or a teaching unit may not be sufficient to determine whether the material will actually help students learn that content. What is needed is a manageable process for examining curriculum materials that gets below the surface by focusing intensely on the appropriateness of content and the utility of instructional design.

With funding from the National Science Foundation and in collaboration with hundreds of   K-12 teachers, curriculum specialists, teacher educators, scientists, and materials developers, Project 2061 of the American Association for the Advancement of Science (AAAS) has been developing a process for analyzing curriculum materials. Field tests suggest that Project 2061's curriculum-analysis procedure will not only serve the materials adoption needs of the schools but also help teachers revise existing materials to increase their effectiveness, guide developers in the creation of new materials, and contribute to the professional development of those who use it.

Specific Learning Goals Are Key

Until recently, there was nothing against which to judge appropriateness of content and utility of instructional design. Now, as a result of the standards-based reform movement in education, these judgments can be made with a high degree of confidence. In mathematics, for example, the appearance of *Science for All Americans* (AAAS, 1989), *Curriculum and Evaluation Standards for School Mathematics* (National Council of Teachers of Mathematics, 1989), and *Benchmarks for Science Literacy* (AAAS, 1993) has made it possible to make more thoughtful decisions about curriculum materials than ever before.

Although the Project 2061 curriculum-analysis procedure was developed using the learning goals in Benchmarks and the mathematics and science standards, subsequent work has indicated that some state education frameworks also can be used. Indeed, the process would seem to apply to any K-12 school subject for which specific learning goals have been agreed upon. These goals must be explicit statements of what knowledge and skills students are expected to learn, and they must be precise. Vague statements such as "students should understand fractions" are not adequate. Instead, consider this benchmark dealing with the meanings of fractions that students should know by the end of the eighth grade:

Students should know that the expression *a/b* can mean different things: a parts of size 1/b each, a divided by b, or a compared to b.

At its simplest level, the Project 2061 curriculum-analysis procedure involves the following five steps:

- Identify specific learning goals to serve as the intellectual basis for the analysis. This is done before beginning to examine any curriculum materials. The source for appropriate goals can be national standards or documents such as those mentioned above, state or local standards and curriculum frameworks, or sources like them. To be useful, the goals must be precise in describing the knowledge or skills they intend students to have. If the set of goals is large, a representative sample of them should be selected for purposes of analysis.

- Make a preliminary inspection of the curriculum materials to see whether they are likely to address the targeted learning goals. If there appears to be little or no correspondence, the materials can be rejected without further analysis. If the outlook is more positive, go on to a content analysis.

- Analyze the curriculum materials for alignment between content and the selected learning goals. The purpose here is to determine, citing evidence from the materials, whether the content in the material matches specific learning goals not just whether the topic headings are similar. At the topic level, alignment is never difficult, since most topics: proportions, equations, graphing, and so forth lack specificity, making them easy to match. If the results of this analysis are positive, then reviewers can take the next step.

- Analyze the curriculum materials for alignment between instruction and the selected learning goals. This involves estimating the degree to which the materials (including their accompanying teacher's guides) reflect what is known generally about student learning and effective teaching and, more important, the degree to which they support student learning of the specific knowledge and skills for which a content match has been found. Again, evidence from the materials must be shown.

- Summarize the relationship between the curriculum materials being evaluated and the selected learning goals. The summary can take the form of a profile of the selected goals in terms of the content and instruction criteria, or a profile of the criteria in terms of the selected goals. In either case, a statement of strengths and weaknesses should be included. With this information in hand, reviewers can make more knowledgeable adoption decisions and suggest ways for improving the examined materials.

In addition to its careful focus on matching content and instruction to very specific learning goals, the Project 2061 procedure has other features that set it apart. For example, its emphasis on collecting explicit evidence (citing page numbers and other references) of a material's alignment with learning goals adds rigor and reliability to decisions about curriculum materials. Similarly, the Project 2061 procedure calls for a team approach to the analytical task, thus providing opportunities for reviewers to defend their own judgments about materials and to question those of other reviewers. These and other characteristics help make participation in the analytical process itself a powerful professional development experience.

The Project 2061 Curriculum-Analysis Procedure in Detail

To provide a better sense of how the procedure works, the following describes in more detail each step in the procedure. The description pays particular attention to the various criteria used to evaluate the instructional effectiveness of materials.

Identify specific learning goals to serve as the intellectual basis for the analysis. After reviewers have agreed upon a set of learning goals as a framework for the analysis, the task is then to choose specific learning goals that will serve as the focus of further study.

When evaluating stand-alone curriculum units that cover a relatively short period of time, it might be possible and worthwhile to analyze all of the learning goals that appear to be targeted by the material. However, in the evaluation of year-long courses or multi-year programs, this becomes impractical. Therefore, a crucial step in the analysis procedure is the sampling of a few learning goals that will lead to valid and reliable generalizations about the material.

Sampling of standards should be representative of the whole set of goals specified in the framework or standards being applied and should reflect the reviewers' needs. For example, if the review committee's task is to select a course in high school Algebra that is aligned with a state mathematics framework or NCTM *Standards*, it might identify a sample of learning goals from important topic areas (e.g., number systems, equations, graphs, functions) and include learning goals that reflect different types of knowledge (e.g., skills, conceptual understanding, problem solving). When examining elementary or middle-school mathematics materials, one would probably want to broaden the range of learning goal statements examined to include important strands in mathematics (e.g., number, geometry, algebra, statistics).

Make a preliminary inspection of the curriculum materials to see whether they are likely to address the targeted learning goals. Once learning goal statements have been selected, the next step is to make a first pass at the materials to identify those whose content appears to correspond reasonably well to the learning goals. Materials that do not meet these initial criteria are not analyzed further.

Reviewers then examine materials on the shortened list more carefully to locate and record places where each selected learning goal seems to be targeted (e.g., particular readings, experiments, discussion questions). If several sightings are found for some or all of the sample learning goals in the material, then these sightings will be looked at more carefully in subsequent steps of the analysis. If, on the other hand, sightings cannot be found for a significant number of the sample learning goals, then the material is dropped from the list.

Analyze the curriculum materials for alignment between content and the selected learning goals. This analysis is a more rigorous examination of the link between the subject material and the selected learning goals and involves giving precise attention to both ends of the match the precise meaning of the learning goal on one end and the precise intention of the material on the other.

With respect to each of the sampled learning goals, the material is examined using such questions as:

- Does the content called for in the material address the substance of a specific learning goal or only the learning goal's general "topic"?

- Does the content reflect the level of sophistication of the specific learning goal, or are the activities more appropriate for targeting learning goals at an earlier or later grade level?

- Does the content address all parts of a specific learning goal or only some? (While it is not necessary that any particular unit would address all of the ideas in a learning goal or standard, the K-12 curriculum as a whole should do so. The purpose of this question is to provide an account of precisely what ideas are treated.)

In addition, an attempt is made to estimate the degree of overlap between the material's content and the set of learning goals of interest. Thus, this step in the analysis is designed to answer questions regarding the material's inclusion of content that is not required for reaching mathematics literacy and the extent to which the material distinguishes between essential and non-essential content. (While distinguishing content essential for literacy from non-essential content in material might seem to be a luxury, it assists teachers in determining the range of students for which the material can be used. Identifying the non-essential material makes it easier for the teacher to direct better students to enrichment activities and allows students themselves to avoid overload from ideas that go beyond what is vital.)

Analyze the curriculum materials for alignment between instruction and the selected learning goals. The purpose here is to estimate how well material addresses targeted learning goals from the perspective of what is known about student learning and effective teaching. The criteria for making the judgments in the instructional analysis are derived from research on learning and teaching and on the craft knowledge of experienced educators. In the context of mathematics literacy, these are summarized in Chapter 13, "Effective Learning and Teaching," of *Science for All Americans*; in Chapter 15, "The Research Base," of *Benchmarks for Science Literacy*.

From these and other sources, seven criteria clusters (shown below) have been identified to serve as a basis for the instructional analysis (for the specific questions within each cluster, see "How to Do Mathematics Curriculum Materials Analysis" on the Project 2061 web site (http://project2061.aaas.org). The proposition here is that (1) the analysis would tie the instruction to each one of the sample learning goals rather than look at instructional strategies globally and (2) in the ideal case, all questions within each cluster would be well-addressed in any material.

Cluster I. Providing a Sense of Purpose: Part of planning a coherent curriculum involves deciding on its purposes and on which learning experiences will likely contribute to those purposes. But while coherence from the curriculum designers' point of view is important, it may not give students an adequate sense of what they are doing and why. This cluster includes criteria to determine whether the material attempts to make its purposes explicit and meaningful to students, either by itself or by instructions to the teacher.

Cluster II. Taking Account of Student Ideas: Fostering better understanding in students requires taking time to attend to the ideas they already have, both ideas that are incorrect and ideas that can serve as a foundation for subsequent learning. Such attention requires that teachers be informed about prerequisite ideas/skills needed for understanding a learning goal and what their students' initial ideas are in particular, the ideas that may interfere with learning the scientific information. Moreover, teachers can help address students' ideas if they know what is likely to work. This cluster examines whether the material contains specific suggestions for identifying and relating to student ideas.

Cluster III. Engaging Students with Mathematical Ideas: Much of the point of mathematics is finding patterns and modeling ideas and relationships in terms of a small number of generalizations or ideas. For students to appreciate the power of mathematics, they need to have a sense of the range and complexity of ideas and applications that mathematics can explain or model. "Students need to get acquainted with the things around them—including devices, organisms, materials, shapes, and numbers—and to observe them, collect them, handle them, describe them, become puzzled by them, ask questions about them, argue about them, and then try to find answers to their questions." (Science for All Americans, p. 201) Furthermore, students should see that the need to explain comes up in a variety of contexts.

Cluster IV. Developing and Using Mathematical Ideas: *Science for All Americans* includes in its definition of mathematics literacy a number of important yet quite abstract ideas—e.g., symbolic representation, patterns and relationships, summarizing data. Such ideas cannot be readily discovered in the real world; the ideas themselves were developed over many hundreds of years as a result of considerable discussion and debate about the existence and logic of laws of mathematics and proofs of theorems. Mathematics literacy requires that students see the link between concepts and skills, see mathematics itself as logical and useful, and become skillful at using mathematics. This cluster includes criteria to determine whether the material expresses and develops ideas in ways that are accessible and intelligible to students, and to demonstrate the usefulness of the concepts and skills in varied contexts.

Cluster V. Promoting Student Thinking About Concepts, Procedures, and Knowledge: No matter how clearly materials may present ideas, students (like all people) will make their own meaning out of it. Constructing meaning well is aided by having students make their ideas and reasoning explicit, hold them up to scrutiny, and recast them as needed. This cluster includes criteria for whether the material suggests how to help students express, think about, and reshape their ideas to make better sense of the world.

Cluster VI. Assessing Progress: There are several important reasons for monitoring student progress toward specific learning goals. Having a collection of alternatives can ease the creative burden on teachers and increase the time available to analyze student responses and make adjustments in instruction based on those responses. This cluster includes criteria for evaluating whether the material includes a variety of goal-relevant assessments.

reprinted with permission from the American Association for the Advancement of Science

Cluster VII. Enhancing the Learning Environment: Many other important considerations are involved in the selection of curriculum materials for example, the help they provide to teachers in encouraging student curiosity and creating a classroom community where all can succeed, or the material's scientific accuracy or attractiveness. The criteria listed in this cluster provide reviewers with the opportunity to comment on these and other important features.

Summarize the relationship between the curriculum materials being evaluated and the selected learning goals. In the preliminary inspection, a few learning goals were selected as representative of the set of goals that the material appears to target. Having analyzed whether the content in the material matches these specific learning goals and how well the instructional strategies in the material support students learning these learning goals, the final step in the process is to provide a profile of the material based on this analysis.

The analysis makes it possible to produce two sets of profiles. The first illustrates how well the material treats each learning goal (for which a content match was found) across all criteria examined in the instructional analysis. Based on these profiles, conclusions can be made about what the material under consideration can be expected to accomplish in terms of learning goals. For example, the profiles may indicate that the material treats one of the examined learning goals well and the rest only moderately or poorly.

The second set of profiles illustrates how well the material meets each criterion in the instructional analysis tool across all learning goals examined. These profiles point to major strengths and weaknesses in the instructional design of the material. For example, the profiles may indicate that the material consistently includes appropriate experiences with phenomena relevant to the learning goals but only occasionally provides students with opportunities to reflect on these experiences. Depending on the time available and their interests, a review committee could decide to produce either one or both sets of profiles. Profiles of different materials provide the basis for selection decisions.

U.S. Department of Education
Expert Panel on Mathematics and Science Education

Evaluation Criteria

A. Quality of Program

Criterion 1. *The program's learning goals are challenging, clear, and appropriate for the intended student population.*

Indicator a.   The program's learning goals are explicit and clearly stated.

Indicator b.   The program's learning goals are consistent with research on teaching and learning or with identified successful practices.

Indicator c.   The program's learning goals foster the development of skills, knowledge, and understandings.

Indicator d.   The program's learning goals can include important concepts within the subject area.

Indicator e.   The program's learning goals can be met with appropriate hard work and persistence.

Criterion 2. *The program's content is aligned with its learning goals, and is accurate and appropriate for the intended student population.*

Indicator a.   The program's content is aligned with its learning goals.

Indicator b.   The program's content emphasizes depth of understanding, rather than breadth of coverage.

Indicator c.   The program's content reflects the nature of the field and the thinking that mathematicians use.

Indicator d.   The program's content makes connections within the subject area and between disciplines.

Indicator e.   The program's content is culturally and ethnically sensitive, free of bias, and reflects diverse participation and diverse student interests.

Criterion 3. *The program's instructional design is appropriate, engaging, and motivating for the intended student population.*

Indicator a. The program's instructional design provides students with a relevant rationale for learning this material.

Indicator b. The program's instructional design attends to students' prior knowledge and commonly held conceptions.

Indicator c. The program's instructional design fosters the use and application of skills, knowledge, and understandings.

Indicator d. The program's instructional design is engaging and promotes learning.

Indicator e. The program's instructional design promotes student collaboration, discourse, and reflection.

Indicator f. The program's instructional design promotes multiple and effective approaches to learning.

Indicator g. The program's instructional design provides for diverse interests.

Criterion 4. *The program's system of assessment is appropriate and designed to inform student learning and to guide teachers' instructional decision.*

Indicator a. The program's system of assessment is an integral part of instruction.

Indicator b. The program's system of assessment is consistent with the content, goals, and instructional design of the program.

Indicator c. The program's system of assessment encourages multiple approaches and makes use of diverse forms and methods of assessment.

Indicator d. The program's system of assessment probes students' abilities to demonstrate depth, flexibility, and application of learning.

Indicator e. The program's system of assessment provides information on students' progress and learning needs.

Indicator f. The program's system of assessment helps teachers select or modify activities to meet learning needs.

B. Usefulness to Others

Criterion 5. *The program can be successfully implemented, adopted, or adapted in multiple educational settings.*

Indicator a. The program provides clear instructions and sufficient training materials to ensure use by those not in the original program.

Indicator b. The program is likely to be successfully transferred to other settings.

Indicator c. The program specifies the conditions and resources needed for implementation.

Indicator d. The program's costs (time and money) can be justified by the benefits.

C. Educational Significance

Criterion 6. *The program's learning goals reflect the vision promoted in national standards in mathematics education.*

Indicator a. The program's learning goals and subject matter content are consistent with national standards.

Indicator b. The program's pedagogy and assessment are aligned with national standards.

Indicator c. The program promotes equity and equal access to knowledge, as reflected in national standards.

Criterion 7. *The program addresses important individual and societal needs.*

Indicator a. The program is of sufficient scope and importance to make a significant difference in student learning.

Indicator b. The program contributes to increases in teachers' knowledge of effective teaching and learning.

Indicator c. The program:

- is designed to improve learning for a wide spectrum of students *OR*

- serves to meet the special learning needs of under-served students *OR*

- serves to meet the special learning needs of students whose interests and talents go beyond core mathematics education.

D. Evidence of Effectiveness and Success

Criterion 8. The program makes a measurable difference in student learning.

Promising Programs, in addition to satisfying Criteria 1–7, must provide **preliminary evidence** of effectiveness in **one or more sites** for **at least one** of the indicators below:

Indicator a. The program has evidence of gains in student understanding of mathematics.

Indicator b. The program has evidence of gains in inquiry, reasoning, and problem solving skills.

Indicator c. The program has evidence of improvements in course enrollments, graduation rates, and post-secondary school attendance.

Indicator d. The program has evidence of improvements in attitudes toward learning.

Indicator e. The program has evidence of narrowing the gap in achievement or accomplishment between disaggregated groups.

Indicator f. The program has other evidence of effectiveness or success.

Exemplary Programs, in addition to satisfying Criteria 1–7, must provide **convincing** evidence of effectiveness in **multiple sites with multiple populations** regarding **two or more** of the indicators below. The items must include either both indicators from Part I or one indicator from Part I and one indicator from Part II. Providing evidence of two indicators from Part II is not sufficient.

Part I

Indicator a. The program has evidence of gains in student understanding of mathematics.

Indicator b. The program has evidence of gains in inquiry, reasoning, and problem solving skills.

Part II

Indicator c. The program has evidence of improvements in course enrollments, graduation rates, and post-secondary school attendance.

Indicator d. The program has evidence of improvements in attitudes toward learning.

Indicator e. The program has evidence of narrowing the gap in achievement or accomplishment between disaggregated groups.

Indicator f. The program has other evidence of effectiveness or success.

CHOOSING A STANDARDS-BASED MATHEMATICS CURRICULUM

Lynn T. Goldsmith

June Mark

Ilene Kantrov

K-12 Mathematics Curriculum Center

Education Development Center, Inc.

HEINEMANN

Portsmouth, NH

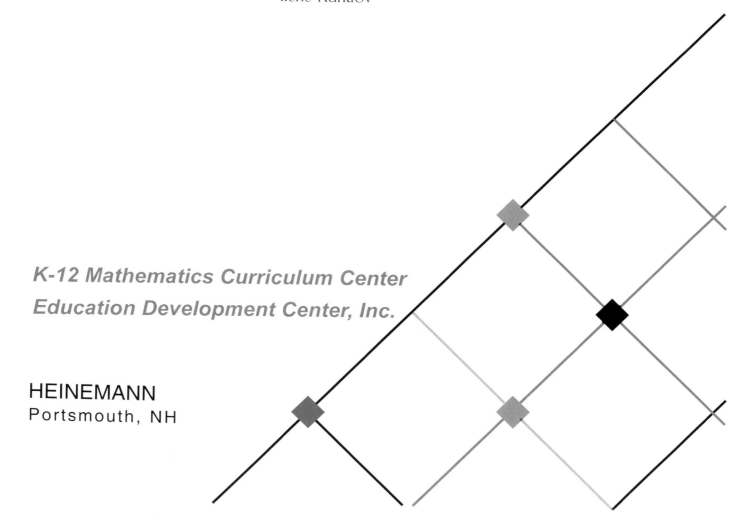

Established in 1997 by Education Development Center, Inc., the K–12 Mathematics Curriculum Center (K–12 MCC) supports school districts as they build effective mathematics education programs using curricula that respond to and align with the National Council of Teachers of Mathematics' *Curriculum and Evaluation Standards for School Mathematics*. The K–12 MCC receives support from the National Science Foundation (NSF) and works with the three NSF-funded grade-level mathematics implementation centers (see Appendix 1).

The K–12 Mathematics Curriculum Center offers a variety of products and services to assist district leadership teams with curriculum selection and implementation. We offer a series of three seminars nationwide; the seminars address the selection and implementation of new curricula, professional development for successful implementation, and leadership for curriculum change.

Additionally, the K–12 MCC provides many print resources, including: *Curriculum Summaries*, providing key at-a-glance information about the 13 NSF-funded comprehensive curricula; a collection of *Curriculum Perspectives* from teachers and administrators who have used the 13 reform curricula; this guide, *Choosing a Standards-Based Mathematics Curriculum*,; a series of short *Issues Papers* that explore contemporary issues in mathematics education; *Discussion Cases* and facilitator guides which parallel the topics of the seminars; *Curriculum Connections*, a newsletter which provides curriculum and resource updates, feature articles, and upcoming seminar information; and a *Curriculum Reader*, which compiles literature pertaining to the consideration of reform mathematics programs.

Another offering of the K–12 MCC is our web site <http://www.edc.org/mcc>, which contains up-to-date information about the Center, the 13 curriculum programs, upcoming events, and resources; and links to other useful sites.

For more information about any of our materials and services, please feel free to contact us:

Ki McClennan
K–12 Mathematics Curriculum Center
Education Development Center, Inc.
55 Chapel Street
Newton, MA 02458-1060
phone: (800) 332-2429
fax: (617) 969-1527
email: mcc@edc.org

HEINEMANN
A Division of Reed Elsevier Inc.
361 Hanover Street
Portsmouth, NH 03801-3912
www.heinemann.com

Offices and agents throughout the world

First published in 1998 by Education Development Center, Inc.

Library of Congress Cataloging-in-Publication Data

Goldsmith, Lynn T., 1950– .
  Choosing a standards-based mathematics curriculum / Lynn T. Goldsmith, June Mark, Ilene Kantrov.
    p. cm.
  Originally published: Newton, MA : Education Development Center, 1998.
  Includes bibliographical references.
  ISBN 0-325-00163-4
  1. Mathematics–Study and teaching–Standards–United States. 2. Curriculum planning–United States. I. Mark, June. II. Kantrov, Ilene. III. Title.
QA13.G65   2000
510'.71–dc21   00-039571

Printed in the United States of America on acid-free paper
08 07 06 05 EB 5 6 7 8 9

Cover design: Jeanine Merrigan, Emily Passman; **cover photos:** Marlene Nelson

This book was developed by the K–12 Mathematics Curriculum Center at Education Development Center, Inc. The work was supported by National Science Foundation grant No. ESI-9617783. Opinions expressed are those of the authors and not necessarily those of the Foundation.